CYBERISH

Author

Rakhi R Wadhwani

Become
Shakespeare
.com

First published in 2019 by

Becomeshakespeare.com

Wordit Content Design & Editing Services Pvt Ltd
Unit - 26, Building A -1, Nr Wadala RTO,
Wadala (East), Mumbai 400037, India
T: +91 8080226699

ISBN - 978-93-88930-81-9

Dedication

I dedicate this book to My Spiritual Guru, My Strong Pillar, My Source of Inspiration, Wisdom, Knowledge and Understanding. He has been the Source of my Strength throughout this journey and on HIS wings only have I soared.

To my Mother, who has encouraged me all the way and whose encouragement has made sure that I give it all it takes to finish that which I have started.

To my Father, who have always loved me unconditionally and whose examples have taught me to work hard for the things that I aspire to achieve.

To my sister and brother-in-law, who has been a constant source of support and encouragement.

To my nephew, who have been affected in every way possible by this quest.

To my spiritual sisters, my mentor, my pillar of strength.

Finally,

To the lovers of books…

I would love to see your book in the hands of people across the world…readers walking down the street, browsers in the bookstores etc.

This is a great challenge, might be not possible to achieve too however it is worth an attempt, even several attempts.

So, take your time, read the book and enjoy.

Thank You. My love for you all can never by quantified.

Legal Notice

Every effort has been made to avoid errors or omissions in this book, however errors may creep in, any mistake, error, or discrepancy noted may be brought to our notice which shall be taken care in the next edition. It is notified that neither the publisher or the author or the seller will be responsible for any damages or loss of action to any one, of any kind, in the manner, there from. It is suggested that to avoid any doubt the reader should cross check all the facts, law and contents of the publication with original Government publication and / or notification.

This book does not provide / offer legal or other advice and should not be relied upon for legal advice. Neither the publisher or the author or the seller does not accept any liability to any person who does rely on the content of this book.

This book is for information purposes only. Nothing in this book constitutes a binding offer to perform any legal service in any jurisdiction.

Reference - National Cyber Safety and Security Standards (https://www.ncdrc.res.in)

Foreword

Every crime that takes place has a cyber component to it, whether it is a petty crime such as theft or a complex one involving cryptocurrencies. With nearly 4 billion internet users (as of 2018 figures) which is doubling every year and ease of access to the every evolving digital gadgets, the crime rate is sure to increase. Recent studies have estimated a figure of 6 trillion dollars as a cost for the cyber crimes by 2021. Due to lack of international laws and treaties the cyber criminals are indulging in these activities without fear. Every country has cyber laws to tackle cyber related crimes, but due to the inherent nature of internet (boundary less) it is difficult for the law enforcement agencies to bring culprits to book.

Cybercrime is not only a concern for the nation states but also to every individual who uses internet which is more of a necessity than a luxury as on date. With in coming of Internet of Things (IoT) and all devices getting connected to each other, the complexity is going to increase more. Financial crimes are on increase as no physical presence is required to commit the crime and behind the anonymity of the internet it is very difficult to put the man behind the machine.

In this book the author explains the various types of crime generally committed via a digital gadget connected to the internet. The author deems this knowledge essential to combat the recent surge in internet-related offences. The prime objective of this book, '**Cyberish**' is to give readers a basic understanding of this issue. Content though technical, the writing style is clear and concise which is simple to understand. The book covers Cyber-pornography, Identity Theft, Hacking, and Criminal Justice & Cyberspace. Also included are reviews of additional studies conducted by other cyber criminologists. The author suggests that future efforts should be undertaken to safeguard information that is frequently stored on electronic media. Overall, this book is designed for every individual who are looking for a quick introduction to the topic of cyber crime. In such a fluid cyber threat scenario, this book will act as an effective guide for all of us understand the dynamics of digital world with changing social values, netiquettes and cyber sanskar. The book will also act as effective tool for empowerment of children; guide them to understand the basics of defence in border less cyber space.

I would like to compliment Rakhi for this initiative, I am sure this will act as a mile stone for digital grooming of our children and future cyber soldiers. I recommend this book to those that want to increase their understanding of this interesting and often confusing topic. Efforts have been made for making a broad and developing subject less perplexing.

- Santosh Khadsare

About Santosh Khadsare

Mr. Santosh Khadsare is an Information Security professional who specializes in Digital Forensics and is currently working as Scientist 'E' in CERT-In (Cyber Forensics), Ministry of Electronics and Information Technology (MeitY), (Government of India) since Feb 2019. He is a B.E (Electronics and Telecommunications) and possesses additional qualifications such as CHFI, CEH, RHCSA, Advance Cyber Forensic Course (CDAC), Cyber Crime Investigator, and Access Data Certified Professional. He has 19+ years plus of rich experience in the field of Information Security, Digital Forensics, Cyber Audit, Cyber Laws and Incident Response. He has been a speaker in various international conferences such as International Conference on Cyber Law, Cybercrime & Cyber Security, C0C0N, HAKON, National Cyber Defense Summit and GovInfoSec Summit Asia. He has also authored various articles on information security and Digital Forensics in national and international publications. He also won the COMMUNITY STAR award at NULLCON International Cyber Security Conference 2017.

Contents

Preface

The Internet's rapid diffusion and digitization of economic activities have led to the emergence of a new breed of criminals. Economic, political, and social impacts of these cyber criminals' activities have received considerable attention in recent years. Individuals, businesses, and governments rightfully worry about the security of their systems, networks, and IT infrastructures.

Looking at the patterns of cybercrimes, it is apparent that many underlying assumptions about crimes are flawed, unrealistic, and implausible to explain this new form of criminality. The empirical records regarding crime patterns and strategies to avoid and fight crimes run counter to the functioning of the cyberworld.

The fields of hacking and cybercrime have also undergone political, social, and psychological metamorphosis. The cybercrime industry is a comparatively young area of inquiry. While there has been an agreement that the global cybercrime industry is tremendously huge, little is known about its exact size and structure. Very few published studies have examined economic and institutional factors that influence strategies and behaviors of various actors associated with the cybercrime industry. Theorists are also debating as to the best way to comprehend the actions of cyber criminals and hackers and the symbiotic relationships they have with various players.

Cybercrime is also a topic of considerable interest both theoretically and practically. This book aims to contribute to resolve the doubts arising in the mind of the common man by simplying the legal aspects / language. A major goal of the book is to explain various cyber crimes, the law associated with it along with punishment and remedies. The book would help us better understand cybercrime as a form of economic activity and could inform the development of strategies for crime prevention.

This book is inter-disciplinary in focus, orientation, and scope. This book is also theory-based, but practical and accessible to the wider audience. This book is primarily targeted to academic specialists, practitioners, professionals, and policy makers interested in and concerned about the evolution of cybercrime industry. Undergraduate and graduate students are also target audience.

More broadly, this book is expected to be useful to all members of the cyberworld to understand the nature of vulnerabilities from cyberattacks and develop appropriate defense mechanisms.

As for the ideas, concepts, content, and theories presented in this book, I am indebted and grateful to several people for comments, suggestion, support, encouragement, and feedbacks.

~Rakhi R Wadhwani

Historical Development of Cyber Crimes

Boundaries of acceptable and ethical behavior in cyberspace yet to be standardized. Neither exists consensus on types of information which can and should be considered property on the network and what constitutes theft or interference with this property.

Cybercrime has its origin in growing dependence on computers in modern life. There exists a wide range of offences committed through communication technology. Routinely, cybercrimes could be categorized in various forms, committing new offences by usage of new technologies like cybercrimes against computer systems and data and secondly, committing old offences by using new technology like using computer network for facilitating the commission of a cybercrime.

History of Cyber Crimes:

Cybercrime has a short but highly eventful history. It is said that with the arrival of computers as with invention of the first Abacus, people used calculating machines for wrong purposes, hence it can be rightly said that cybercrime per se in different forms has been around ever. Literally history of cybercrimes initially commenced with hackers trying to break into computer networks just only for the thrill of accessing high level security networks or to gain sensitive or secured information or any secret for personal benefits or for revenge.

Exact origin of cybercrime, the very supposedly first instance in which someone committed a crime across a computer network isn't possible to authenticate. But the first major attack on a digital network is possible, which can be used as a reference point of event in the evolution of cyber based crimes.

A brief historical development of cybercrime in the use of computers and computer networks follows:

It's but difficult to determine the first crime involving a computer, as gathering of information and mechanical cryptographic system can be tracked beyond 5,000 years. Early computer crimes involved subversion of long-distance telephone networks and physical damages to computer systems. In 1900 B.C., encryption and decryption system of information was in existence used by an Egyptian. Later Julius Caesar used a normal alphabet in government communications in 100-44 B.C. for the purpose of maintaining information security. Attempts made to find out early history of cybercrimes from the phase of 1820's.

1820: First recorded cybercrime took place in the year 1820. That is not surprising considering the fact that abacus, which is thought to be the earliest form of computer has been around since 3500 B.C. in India, Japan and China. Era of modern computers, however, began with the analytical engine of Charles Babbage. In 1820, Joseph-Marie Jacquard, a textile manufacturer in France, produced the loom. This device allowed the repetition of a series of steps in weaving of special fabrics. Thus, resulting in a fear amongst Jacquard's employees that their traditional employment and livelihood were being threatened, they committed acts of sabotage to discourage

Jacquard from further use of new technology. This is known as the first recorded cybercrime in the history.

Admittedly, physical damages to computer systems and subversion of long-distance telephone networks were involved in the early computer crimes.

U.S. is birthplace of the Internet and first computer facilitated crime in the year **1969**. During 1960s and 1970s, a litany of early physical attacks on computer systems was catalogued by Thomas Whiteside.

Cyber criminals involved in telephone Phreakers became hackers in 1960s as they had excess curiosity to know about computers, computer systems and its use for their own ends in the early 1960s. They went on their work to learn the change of computer codes of the system. But in early stages of this new technology crimes were committed by technology experts who directly attacked into computers, computer system or computer networks.

February 1969, the largest student riot in Canada was set off, police were called in to put an end to the student occupation of several floors of the Hall Building. These students were protesting against a professor accused of racism, when police arrived. Fire broke in resulting in computer data and university property damaged and destroyed. The damages totaled $2 million and 97 people were arrested.

1970: Malicious association became evident with the purpose of hacking and at those times computerized phone systems were targeted. They were associated with purpose to directly damage computer centers. At the time, German state of Hesse enacted the world 1st computer specific law in the form of **Data Protection Act, 1970** with new cyber technology. With passage of time, technology emerged with misuse options with a dire necessity for stricter statutory laws of regulating activities in the cyber world.

By 1970, cyber worldwide network was open to worldwide users, what evolved as cybercrime was and became a lethal legal challenge worldwide was **Cyber Pornography.**

1971: John Draper, a phone Phreaker, discovers that a whistle given out as a prize in boxes of Cap'n Crunch cereal produced the same tones as telephone switching computers of the time. Phone phreak is a term used to describe computer programmers obsessed with phone networks, the basis of modern-day computer networking. He built a "blue box" with the whistle that would allow him to make free long-distance phone calls and then published instructions on how to make it. The instances of wire fraud rose significantly.

1972: The **Inter Networking Group** founded to govern standards for Internet usage.

1973: A teller at a local New York bank used a computer to embezzle over $2 million dollars.

1976: Whitfield Diffie and Martin Hellman introduced the idea of public key cryptography to adopt security standard software to prevent and control computer misuse.

1977: In the USA, Ronald L. Rivest, Leonard M. Adleman and Adi Shamir also introduced new software for **public key cryptography** and **digital signature.** Till the end of 1980s even the concept of personal computers (PCs) were not known to them. Therefore, at that time in Russia programmers and hackers were attached to computer centers and cyber cafes. They used to work in the same place closely to make brand name e.g. IBM, DEC, operating system, software packaging. Hackers started using programme code. The Russian Government employed those programmers for security measures in the late 1960s and 1970s.

1978: The first electronic **Bulletin Board System (BBS)** came online and quickly became a preferred method of communication for the cyber world. It allowed fast, free exchange of knowledge including tips and tricks for hacking into computer networks.

1981: Ian Murphy, known as Captain Zap to his fans, was the **first person convicted of a cybercrime.** He hacked into the AT&T network and changed the internal clock to charge off-hours rates at peak times. He received 1000 hours of community service and 2.5 years of probation, as compared to today's penalties. He was also an inspiration for the **movie Sneakers.**

1981-1982: Elk Cloner, a virus, is written as a joke by a 15-year-old kid. The first virus exposed to the world what came into being before the experimental work which defines viruses of contemporary world. It is one of the first known viruses to leave its original operating system and spread in the "wild". It attacked Apple II operating systems and spread by floppy disk.

1983: The **first documented experimental virus** was conceived to be presented at a weekly seminar for computer security by the author and the name "virus" by Len Adleman.

1983: The movie **War Games** is released and brings hacking to the mainstream. The movie depicts a teenage boy who hacks into a government computer system through a back door and nearly brings the world to World War III.

1984: Fred Cohen **defines computer virus** as a computer programme that can affect other computer programmes by modifying them in such a way as to include a possibly evolved copy of itself.

1986: Brain and Virdem, two Pakistani's developed a method of infecting it with a virus they dubbed "Brain" which could infect 360 kb floppy with "©Brain" for a volume label. They also widely spread this virus on MS-DOS P system. It is called that this was the **first file virus** which was created in this year.

1986: The systems administrator at the Lawrence Berkeley National Laboratory, Clifford Stoll, noted certain irregularities in accounting data. Inventing the **first digital forensic techniques,** he determined that an unauthorized user was hacking into his computer network. Stoll used what is called a "**honey pot tactic**" which lures a hacker back into a network until enough data can be collected to track the intrusion to its source. Stoll's effort paid off with the eventual arrest of Markus Hess and a number of others located in West Germany, who were stealing and selling military information, passwords and other data.

1986: Congress passes the **Computer Fraud and Abuse Act,** making hacking and theft illegal but there was the weakness of this law of not covering juveniles under its purview.

1988: Robert T. Morris jr., a graduate student at Cornell, released a self-replicating worm onto the Defense Department's **ARPANET**. ARPANET is the precursor to the Internet as we know it today. The worm got out of hand and infected more than 600,000 networked computers (military sites, medical research sites, installation sites, University websites). The court found him guilty under title **18 USC 1030(a)(5)(A)** and was **sentenced to 3 years of probation, 400 hours of community service, a fine of $10,050** and the costs of his supervision.

1989: The first large scale case of **ransomware** is reported. The virus posed as a quiz on the AIDS virus and once downloaded, help computer data hostage for $500. At the same time another group is arrested stealing US government and private sector data and selling it to the KGB.

1990: The **Electronic Frontier Foundation** was formed.

1990: The Legion of Doom and Masters of Deception, two cyber based gangs, engage in **online warfare.** They actively block each other's connections, hack into computers and steal data. These two groups were large-scale phone phreaks famous for numerous hacks into telephone mainframe infrastructure. The proliferation of the two groups, along with other cyber gangs, led to an FBI sting cracking down on BBS's promoting credit card theft and wire fraud.

1990: United Kingdom passed the **Computer Misuse Act** but before this enactment the Telecommunication Act, 1984 which prohibits the misuse of public telecommunications network was very significant in scope. United Kingdom Parliament has revised this Act in **1994** and amended in the late **1996.** After revision and amendment, the Act provides for prohibiting the unauthorized access for committing espionage, unauthorized access to non-public government computer, computer fraud, damage to computer, trafficking in passwords, threats to damage a computer etc.

1993: Kevin Poulson is caught and convicted for **hacking into the phone systems.** He took control of all phone lines going into an LA radio station in order to guarantee winning a call-in contest. At one point he was featured on **America's Most Wanted,** when the phone lines for the show went mysteriously silent. When the FBI began their search, he went on the run but was eventually caught. He was sentenced to **5 years in Federa penitentiary** and was **the first to have a ban on Internet use included in his sentence.**

1994: The **World Wide Web** is **launched**, allowing black hat hackers to move their product information from the old Bulletin Board Systems (BBS) to their very own websites. A student in the UK uses the information to hack into Korea's nuclear program, NASA and other US agencies using only a Commodore Amiga personal computer and a "**blueboxing**" program found online.

1995: The **Telegraph Act** was passed in **India.** This Act was further amended with the objective of adopting proper regulations in the cyberspace.

1995: Macro-viruses appear. Macro viruses are viruses written in computer languages embedded within applications. These macros run when the application is opened, such as word processing or spreadsheet documents and are an easy way for hackers to deliver malware. This is why opening unknown email attachments can be very risky. Macro-viruses are still hard to detect and are a leading cause of computer infection.

1996: CIA Director John Deutsh testifies to Congress that foreign based organized crime rings are actively trying to hack US government and corporate networks. The US GAO announced that its files **had been attacked** by hackers at least **650,000 times** and that at least **60%** of them were **successful.**

1997: The FBI reports that over 85% of US companies had been hacked and most don't even know it. The Chaos Computer Club Hack Quicken software was able to make financial transfers without the bank or the account holder knowing about it.

1997: The US Attorney General Janet Reno said that criminals no longer are restricted by national boundaries. If we keep up with cybercrimes, we must work together as never before. After meeting at Federal Bureau of Investigation's headquarters of the Justice Ministers of the G-8 countries, the news released for collaboration of these major countries to:

1. Assign adequate number of properly trained and equipped law enforcement personnel to investigate high tech crimes.
2. Improve ways to track attacks on computer networks.
3. When extradition is not possible, prosecute criminals in the country where they are found.
4. Preserve key evidence on computer networks.
5. Review the legal codes in each nation to ensure that appropriate crimes for computer wrong doing are prescribed and to ensure that the language makes it easier to develop new ways to detect and prevent computer crimes.
6. Increase efforts to use new communication technologies, such as video teleconferencing to obtain testimony from witnesses in other nations.

1997: Alleged transcript of telephonic conversation about the Tata Tea case between Ratan Tata, Nusli Wadia and Field Marshal Sam Manek Shaw are remarkable case of **telephone tapping.**

1997: The Yahoo! Internet search engine was attacked by hackers with the threat to release from prison Kevin Mitnick the so-called popular hacker, otherwise they will send a **"logic bomb"** in the personal computers of Yahoo users on December 25, 1997.

1998: Thousands of fake information requests were received by the Federal Bureau labour statistics due to cyber-attack called **"spamming"** which was developed as new mode of attack by hackers.

1999: The **Melissa Virus is released.** It becomes the most virulent computer infection to date and results in one of the first convictions for someone writing malware. The Melissa virus was a macro-virus with the intention of taking over email accounts and sending out mass-mailings. The virus writer was **accused** of causing more than **$80 million in damages** to computer networks and **sentenced** to **5 years** in prison.

1999: The United States of America passed the **Electronic Communications Privacy Act,** 1999 for the protection of right to privacy. The significant Amendments have been made for cryptography, security and freedom in cyberspace in the Constitution of United States of America. Recently certain statute has also been enacted like **Spyware Control and Privacy Protection Act 2000** (USCs 3180IS) to protect the disclosure of the collection of information through computer, computer software and other related purposes.

Modern History:

Of late criminals that indulge in cybercrimes are not just driven by ego or expertise. Instead, they use their knowledge to gain benefits quickly. They are using their expertise to steal, deceive and exploit people as they find it easy to earn money without having to do an honest day's work. Modern cybercrimes are quite different from old school crimes. These crimes do not require physical presence of the criminals.

The brief modern history of cybercrimes in the use of computers and computer networks are as follows:

2000: The **Parliament of India** passed the **Information Technology Act (ITA), 2000** with the object to combat cybercrimes and to provide a legal framework for e-commerce transactions. In India, this was the very **first cyber legislation** which specifically deals with cybercrimes. It deals with the various types of offences which is done in the electronic form or concerning with computers, computer systems, computer networks. The term "cybercrime" or "cyber offence" is neither defined nor this expression is used under the Information Technology Act, 2000. This Act **amends** many provisions of our existing laws, i.e. **Indian Penal Code, 1860;** the **Indian Evidence Act, 1872,** the **Bankers Book Evidence Act, 1891** and the **Reserve Bank of India Act, 1934.**

2000: The number and types of **online attacks grows exponentially.** Music retailer CD Universe is extorted for millions after its clients' credit card information was published online. Denial of Service (DDoS) attacks is launched, numerous times, against AOL, Yahoo!, Ebay and many others. Fake news causes shares of Emulex stocks to crash nearly 50%. The I Love

You Virus spreads across the internet. Then President Clinton says he doesn't use email to talk with his daughter because the technology isn't secure.

2002: Shadow Crew's website is **launched.** The website was a message board and forum for black hat hackers. Members could post, share and learn how to commit a multitude of cybercrimes and avoid capture. The site lasted for 2 years before being shut down by the Secret Service. 28 people were arrested in the US and 6 other countries.

2003: SQL Slammer becomes the fastest spreading worm in history. It infected SQL servers and created a Denial of Service Attack which affected speeds across the Internet for quite some time. In terms of infection speed, it spread across nearly 75,000 machines in less than 10 minutes.

2004–2005: Data breaches happen on a daily basis with having a negative impact on the attacked business. They can change the security industry and influence legislation in some cases. At that time the cyber scammers had proven their skills and for them it was the good time to move for causing damage and gain money in real sense. By this time the cyber criminals became professionally experts in doing cybercrimes and also for encouraging others for their involvement. That's why this time period is remembered as lure of money and professionalism.

Another important issue of this phase is that cybercrimes were at the advance stage with the development of software which could gain privileged access to a computer while at the same time hiding its presence. Then the cyber crooks started to use this software with the intention to hide malware by stealing passwords and to gain credit card information as well as spreading viruses. By using this trick, the cyber crooks could infect and control thousands of computers remotely at the same time without the knowledge of computer users.

2006-2008: Cybercriminal started organizing into gangs with a growing amount of money at stake. Even some cybercriminals had a Mafia-like structure with malicious hackers, programmers and data sellers reporting to managers and that person in turn reported to a boss who was in charge of distributing cybercrime kits. They could also spread malware just by a hole that the software maker had not closed for the purpose of taking complete control over user's computers. By this time the cyber criminals became professionally experts in doing cybercrimes through their gangs and also for encouraging others for their involvements in the gangs. That's why this time period is remembered as lure of money through gangs and discretion.

2007: The instances of hacking, data theft and malware infections skyrockets. The numbers of records stolen, machines infected rise into the millions, the amount of damages caused into the billions. The Chinese government is accused of hacking into US and other governmental systems.

2009-2010: Known for social networking and engineering because the social networking sites such as Facebook and Twitter started to take off in the later part of the decade. This phase is known for social networking and engineering because the social networking sites such as Facebook and Twitter started to take off in the later part of the decade.

Cyber criminals started to collect the personal information of users with a growing amount of money at stake because users post everything on the sites like from where they lived and worked to their current location. They have also played the game by employing social engineering by finding out the topics of internet user's interest and then post a message or images or videos by mentioning or using that topic with a link to a website which was created with the aim to steal credit card and other personal information for lure of money. By this time the cyber criminals became more experts in doing cybercrimes through connecting with social networking sites.

2010: Google first time publicly announced that it got hit with a cyber-attack called **Operation Aurora;** the search engine giant was hit along with other major organizations such as Adobe Systems, Yahoo and Symantec and launched advanced persistent threats (APTs) into the mainstream. APTs typically refer to a group that persistently targets certain entities and cyber espionage and intelligence to gather sensitive data.

2011-Till Date: The National Crime Records Bureau (NCRB), Ministry of Home Affairs in India has released Cyber Crime Statistics for the year 2013, which again shows rapid increase in cybercrime by 50% on year to year basis from 2012-2013.

The statistics mainly show cases registered under cybercrimes by motives and suspects. The maximum offenders came from the 18-30 age groups. Among states, the highest incidents of cybercrime took place in Maharashtra (907) followed by UP (682) and AP (651).

The maximum cyber-criminal arrested under the IT Act in Maharashtra (426) and AP (296) followed by UP (283).

In percentage terms, the most dramatic increase in cases registered under IT act in Uttarakhand (475%) followed by Assam (450%).

Interestingly, the picture postcard union territory, Andaman and Nicobar Islands, registered an eye-popping increase of 800% in the same category.

Delhi city has registered 131 cases of cybercrime which is an increase of 72.4% as compared to last year 2012; whereas Lakshadweep, Dadra and Nagar Haveli reported no cybercrime cases for the year 2013. Likewise, cybercrime activities seem to be rare in the north eastern. In 2013, only one case each was registered in Nagaland and Mizoram.

Thus, cybercrime has its origin in the growing dependence on computers in modern life. There is a wide range of offences that can be committed through communication technology.

It ain't going to stop and seems like it will just continue to grow until new methods of fighting it are introduced, whereas it is found that at some point of time, history becomes current events.

Currently, it is noticable that due to technology of internet era, there are very few people whose lives aren't affected whether it is beneficially or harmfully. There is also the positive side of this technology as well as negative. By the positive side it is found that there is tremendous increase in the ability to share and exchange information instantaneously which led to provide unprecedented benefits in the areas of education, commerce, entertainment and social interaction and on the negative side, it is felt that there is the increase in opportunities for the commission of crimes because this latest technology has encouraged the potential criminals to commit crimes through computer, computer system or computer network with almost no monetary cost and with lesser risk of being caught.

To compare this latest type of crimes using technology with the perpetrators of traditional economic-motivated crimes like burglaries, larcenies, bank robberies etc.; it is found that cybercrimes are relatively free from worry of directly encountering law enforcement and witnesses. Because in the past decade, this ever-growing technology has altered the way of teenagers to communicate and interact with others like their age friends, youngster, older and parents.

Hacking

What is Hacking?

Hacking refers to activities that seek to compromise digital devices, such as computers, smartphones, tablets and even entire networks. Hackers are motivated by personal gain to make a statement or just because they can.

It means unauthorized control / access over computer system and act of hacking completely destroys the whole data as well as computer programmes. Hackers usually hack telecommunication and mobile network.

Hacking is typically technical in nature but hackers can also use psychology to trick the user into clicking on a malicious attachment or providing personal data which is also known as "**social engineering**".

Hacktivism attacks those included famous Twitter, blogging platform by unauthorized access / control over the computer. Due to hacking activity there will be loss of data as well as computer. Also research especially indicates that those attacks were not mainly intended for financial gain too and to diminish the reputation of particular person or company. A hacker is an unauthorized user who attempts to or gains access to an information system. Hacking is a crime even if there is no visible damage to the system, since it is an invasion in to the privacy of data. There are different classes of Hackers.

Types of Hackers:

- **Ethical Hacker** – Also known as White Hat hacker – gains access to the systems with a view to fix the identified weaknesses by performing penetration testing and vulnerability assessments. They believe that information sharing is good, and that it is their duty to share their expertise by facilitating access to information. However, there are some white hackers who are just "joy riding" on computer systems.
- **Cracker** – Also known as Black Hat hacker – gains unauthorized access to computer systems for personal gain – usually to steal data, personal information, transfer funds from bank accounts etc. They cause damage after intrusion. They may steal or modify data or insert viruses or worms which damage the system.
- **Grey Hat Hacker** – is in between ethical and black hat hackers. Breaks into the systems without authority to identify weaknesses and report them to the system owner.

  Typically, ethical but occasionally violates hacker ethics. Hackers will hack into networks, stand-alone computers and software. Network hackers try to gain unauthorized access to private computer networks just for challenge, curiosity and distribution of information. Crackers perform unauthorized intrusion with damage like stealing or changing of information or inserting malware (viruses or worms).
- **Script Kiddies** – A non-skilled person who gains access to computer systems using readymade hacking tools.
- **Hacktivist** – A hacker who use hacking to send social, religious, political etc. messages which is usually done

by hijacking websites and leaving messages on the hijacked websites.

- **Phreaker** – A hacker who identifies and exploits weaknesses in telephones instead of computers.

Types of Cyber Crime:

- **DDOS Attacks** – This involves the use of computers in multiple locations to attack servers with a view of shutting them down.
- **Botnets** – Scan can be used to perform distributed denial of service attack (DDOS attacks), steal data, send spam and allows the attacker to access the device and its connection.
- **Identity Theft** – Stealing personal information from somebody and impersonating that person.
- **Cyberstalking** – Is a crime in which the attacker harasses a victim using electronic communication, such as e-mail or instant messaging or messages posted to a Web site or a discussion group.
- **Social Engineering** – Is an attack vector that relies heavily on human interaction and often involves manipulating people into breaking normal security procedures and best practices in order to gain access to systems, networks or physical locations or for financial gains.
- **Potentially Unwanted Programs (PUPs)** – Are less threatening than other cybercrimes but are a type of malware.
- **Phishing** - Smart hacking technique used as a baited trap by hackers by sending malicious email attachments or URLs to users to gain access to their accounts or computers to steal data.

- **Prohibited / Illegal Content** - Involves criminals sharing and distributing inappropriate content that can be considered highly distressing and offensive.
- **Online Scams** - Sending unauthorized emails. These emails usually contain advertisements.
- **Exploit Kits** – Readymade tools which a criminal can buy online and use against anyone with a computer. Exploit Kits needs a vulnerability in order to gain control of a user's computer.
- **Computer Fraud** – Intentional deception for personal gain via the use of computer systems.
- **Privacy Violation** – Exposing personal information on social media, websites etc.
- **Sharing copyrighted material** – This involves distributing copyright protected materials.
- **Electronic funds transfer** – This involves gaining an unauthorized access to bank computer networks and making illegal fund transfers.
- **Electronic money laundering** – This involves the use of the computer to launder money.
- **ATM Fraud** – This involves intercepting ATM card details.

Impact of Cybercrime on Society

Cybercrime has created a major threat to those who use the internet, with millions of users' information stolen within the past few years. **IBM president and CEO Ginni Rometty** described cybercrime as "**the greatest threat to every profession, every industry, every company in the world.**"

Read below for shocking statistics on cybercrime impact on our society till date (reference: https://www.pandasecurity.com)

- The global cost of cybercrime will reach **$6 trillion** by 2021.
- *According to the Ponemon Institute's 2016 Cost of Data Breach Study, Global Analysis organizations that suffered at least one breach in 2016 lost an average of $4 million.*
- **48% of data security breaches** are caused by acts of malicious intent.
- Cybersecurity Ventures expects ransomware costs will rise to **$11.5 billion in 2019**.
- Cybercrime – more than **triple the number** of unfilled Cyber Security jobs by 2021.

How to fight Cyber Crime?

Hackers are taking over our systems and no one is safe in the modern age of technology. The average time taken to detect a cyber-breach **is more than 200 days**.

Bad guys, BEWARE and BE AWARE. We have got ways to beat you.

- Become vigilant when browsing websites.
- Report suspicious emails immediately.
- Never click on unfamiliar links or advertisements.
- Ensure websites are secured and safe before entering credentials.
- Keep operating systems and application updated always.
- Use strong passwords.
- Download up-to-date security programs, including anti-malware software with multiple technologies for protecting against spyware, ransom ware and exploits, as well as a firewall.

- Destroy all traces of your personal information on hardware you plan to sell.
- Don't use open Wi-Fi on your router; it makes it too easy for hackers to steal your connection and download illegal files.
- Come up with creative answers for your security questions.
- Keep sensitive data off the cloud. "No matter which way you cut it, data stored on the cloud doesn't belong to you" says Taggart. "There are very few cloud storage solutions that offer encryption for 'data at rest'. Use the cloud storage if it is important else don't.

Section 43A – Compensation for failure to protect data
Where a body corporate, possessing, dealing or handling any sensitive personal data or information in a computer resource which it owns, controls or operates, is negligent in implementing and maintaining reasonable security practices and procedures and thereby causes wrongful loss or wrongful gain to any person, such body corporate shall be liable to pay damages by way of compensation, not exceeding five crore rupees, to the person so affected.

Section 66: Computer Related Offences

If any person, dishonestly, or fraudulently, does any act referred to in section 43, he shall be punishable with imprisonment for a term which may extend to two three years or with fine which may extend to five lakh rupees or with both.

Explanation: For the purpose of this section-

a) the word "dishonestly" shall have the meaning assigned to it in section 24 of the Indian Penal Code;

b) the word "fraudulently" shall have the meaning assigned to it in section 25 of the Indian Penal Code.

Section 66C: Punishment for identity theft

Whoever, fraudulently or dishonestly make use of the electronic signature, password or any other unique identification feature of any other person, shall be punished with imprisonment of either description for a term which may extend to three years and shall also be liable to fine which may extend to rupees one lakh.

IPC Section 379: Punishment for theft

Whoever commits theft shall be punished with imprisonment of either description for a term which may extend to three years, or with fine, or with both.

IPC Section 406: Punishment for criminal breach of trust

Whoever commits criminal breach of trust shall be punished with imprisonment of either description for a term which may extend to three years, or with fine, or with both.

Classification of Offence

Punishment - Imprisonment for 3 years and fine, or both - Compoundable by the owner of the property in respect of which breach of trust has been committed, with the permission of the court.

Illustration 1:

A German citizen recruited by the KGB to spy for the Soviets in the 1980s. Hess was tasked with breaking into U.S. military computers to obtain classified information.

From the University of Bremen in Germany, Hess used the German Datex-P network via satellite link or transatlantic cable to the Tymnet Internation Gateway. He was able to eventually attack 4000 U.S. military computers, including those at military installations in Germany and Japan, as well as machines at MIT in Cambridge, Massachusetts and the OPTIMIS Database at the Pentagon.

Hess's activity was eventually detected by Clifford Stoll, an astronomer turned systems administrator of the computer center of the Lawrence Berkeley Laboratory (LBL) in California. Hess was found guilty of espionage and sentenced to one to three years in prison.

Illustration 2:

As a graduate student at Cornell University in 1988, Robert Morris created what would come to be known as the first worm on the Internet. Morris has said he created the worm not for damage, but to give him an idea of the size of the web. In order to hide the worm's origins at Cornell, Morris released it from MIT, unleashing it to exploit vulnerabilities in Unix sendmail, finger and RSH/REXEC. However, a design flaw caused the worm to replicate itself at higher levels than Morris has intended, overloading systems and causing significant damage.

After he was identified as the source of the worm, Robert Morris became the first person convicted under the Computer Fraud and Abuse Act in 1990. Morris was sentenced to three years of probation, 400 hours of community service, a fine of $10,050 and the costs of his supervision.

Illustration 3:

In what is seen by many as one of the first high-profile instances of financially-motivated hacking, Russian crime ring leader Vladimir Levin managed to gain access to accounts located in the Citibank network and stole millions of dollars in 1995.

Working as part of a larger crime group and using a computer based in London, Levin was able to get a list of customer codes and passwords that allowed him to log in many times over a several-week period and transfer money into accounts controlled by the crime organization. Officials said Levin managed to transfer $3.7 million illegally.

The FBI eventually caught up with Levin at a London airport and he was tried and convicted in the U.S. and sentenced to three years in jail in 1998. He was also ordered to pay Citibank $240,015 in restitution.

Illustration 4:

Known by the hacker name c0mrade, Jonathon James was 16 when, in 1999, he hacked into the Marshall Space Flight Center in Huntsville, Alabama, and downloaded proprietary software for the International Space Station. The software supported the International Space Station's physical environment and was responsible for critical control of humidity and temperature for living in space.

NASA officials valued the documents stolen by James at around $1.7 million. The incident forced NASA to shut down its computer systems for three weeks and cost them about $41,000 to fix.

Illustration 5:

In 2002, at age 19, Adrian Lamo hacked into the internal network of the New York Times and accessed many sensitive records, including an extensive database of op-ed writers the paper had used in the past.

The records contained names and, in some instances, phone numbers, home addresses and payment history of contributors such as Democratic strategist James Carville, former secretary of state James Baker, and (ironically, Sneakers movie veteran) actor Robert Redford. Lamo added his own name to the list of "experts" and under "expertise" he wrote "Computer hacking, national security, communications intelligence."

Illustration 6:

Scottish hacker Gary McKinnon, who went by the handle Solo, was accused of hacking to several US military computers in 2001 and 2002. McKinnon allegedly wanted to know what the government knew about UFOs.

Military officials said the damage caused by McKinnon included the deletion of critical files from operating systems, prompting a shut down the US Army's Military District of Washington network of 2,000 computers for 24 hours. McKinnon also allegedly deleted weapons logs at the Earle Naval Weapons Station. Officials said the cost of clean-up from McKinnon's hack was over $700,000.

Illustration 7:

Albert Gonzalez was the convicted ring leader of a group of cyber criminals which, from 2005 through 2007, stole more than 90 million credit and debit card numbers from TJX and other retailers, including shoe sellers DSW, OfficeMax, BJs Wholesale Club and Dave & Busters. Gonzalez was also the mastermind behind the hacking that caused the massive records breach of Heartland Payment Systems in 2008.

In 2009, Gonzalez was sentenced to two concurrent 20-year prison sentences, the lengthiest sentence ever imposed in the United States for hacking or identity-theft.

Illustration 8:

In early 2011, Antisec group Anonymous got angry when Aaron Barr, at the time the CEO of HB Gary Federal, alluded to plans to reveal the identities of several Anonymous members at the Security B-Sides conference. In retaliation, the group compromised the systems of both HBGary Federal and sister firm HB Gary Inc. Anonymous then copied and made public thousands of private HBGary documents, including emails.

In one of the first events to really bring "hacktivism" to the attention of the mainstream press, it was reported that some of the documents stolen by Anonymous revealed HBGary Federal was working with Bank of America to respond to Wikileaks' planned release of BOA internal documents. The HBGary documents detailed some planned shady tactics, including launching a "dirty tricks" campaign against Wikileaks and disrupting a Salon.com reporter who was assumed to be sympathetic to Wikileaks.

Illustration 9:

An offshoot of Anonymous, hacktivist group Lulzsec in June 2011 hacked into Sony Pictures via SQL Injection attack and stole data that included names, passwords, e-mail and home addresses of thousands of customers.

Lulzsec, saying the attack was retaliation for Sony's legal action against hacker George Hotz for jailbreaking into the PlayStation 3, claimed to have compromised over one million accounts. Sony has claimed the number of compromised accounts was much lower.

Founding Lulzec member Sabu (real name Hector Xavier Monsegur) was arrested by federal agents in June 2011 and agreed to become an FBI informant, providing the FBI with details that lead to the arrest of five other "hacktivists" associated with the groups Anonymous, Lulzsec and Antisec. Sabu himself eventually plead guilty to criminal charges, including multiple counts of conspiracy to engage in computer hacking.

Illustration 10:

Employees of British paper News of the World were found to have hacked into the phones of celebrities, politicians and even murder victims in pursuit of stories for the tabloid.

In an investigation that dated back to 2002, it was eventually revealed that reporters, as well as private investigators hired by the paper, had hacked into the voicemail accounts of celebrities such as model Elle McPherson and actress Sienna Miller, as well as members of the British Royal Family. In one instance, a PI working for the paper had tampered with official police evidence by listening to and inadvertently deleting the voicemails of murdered school girl Milly Dowler.

The 168-year-old paper was eventually shuttered in the wake of the scandal.

Crimes Involving Money

Money is the most common motive behind all crime. The same is also true for cybercrime. Globally it is being observed that more and more cybercrimes are being committed for financial motives rather than for "revenge" or for "fun".

With the tremendous increase in the use of internet and mobile banking, online share trading, dematerialization of shares and securities, this trend is likely to increase unabated. Financial crimes include cyber cheating, credit card frauds, money laundering, hacking, accounting scams etc., into bank servers, computer manipulation.

Section 66D: Punishments for cheating by personation by using computer resource (IT Act 2000)

Whoever, by means of any communication device or computer resource cheats by personation, shall be punished with imprisonment of either description for a term which may extend to three years and shall also be liable to fine which may extend to one lakh rupees.

Section 415 of IPC for any kind of Cheating

Whoever, by deceiving any person, fraudulently or dishonestly induces the person so deceived to deliver any property to any person, or to consent that any person shall retain any property, or intentionally induces the person so deceived to do or omit to do anything which he would not do or omit if he were not so deceived, and which act or omission causes or is likely to cause damage or harm to that person in body, mind, reputation or property, is said to "cheat".

Explanation - A dishonest concealment of facts is a deception within the meaning of this section.

Illustration 1

Rs. 2,50,000 were misappropriated from Bank of Baroda in India through falsification of computerized bank accounts.

Illustration 2

The Hyderabad police in India arrested an unemployed computer operator and his friend, a steward in a prominent five-star hotel, for stealing and misusing credit card numbers belonging to hotel customers.

The steward noted down the various details of the credit cards, which were handed by clients of the hotel for paying their bills. Then, he passed all the details to his computer operator friend who used the details to make online purchases on various websites.

Illustration 3

In 2004, the US Secret Service investigated and shut down an online organization that trafficked in around 1.7 million stolen credit cards and stolen identity information and documents.

This high-profile case, known as "Operation Firewall," focused on a criminal organization of some 4,000 members whose Web site functioned as a hub for identity theft activity.

Illustration 4

In 2003, a hacker was convicted in the USA for causing losses of almost $25 million. The defendant pleaded guilty to numerous charges of conspiracy, computer intrusion, computer fraud, credit card fraud, wire fraud, and extortion.

The hacker and his accomplices from Russia had stolen usernames, passwords, credit card information, and other financial data by hacking into computers of US citizens. They would then extort money from those victims with the threat of deleting their data and destroying their computer systems.

Illustration 5

Punjab National Bank in India was cheated to the tune of Rs. 13.9 million through false debits and credits in computerized accounts.

Case of Extortion of Money through Internet

The complainant has received a threatening email and demanded protection from unknown person claiming to be the member of Halala Gang, Dubai. Police registered a case u/s. 384/506/511 IPC.

The sender of the email used the email ID xyz@yahoo.com & abc@yahoo.com and signed as Chengez Babar.

The Cyber cafes from which the emails have been made were monitored and the accused person was nabbed red handed.

Cyber Pornography and Child Pornography

Cyber pornography is believed to be one of the largest businesses on the Internet today. The millions of pornographic websites that flourish on the Internet are testimony to this. While pornography per se is not illegal in many countries, child pornography is strictly illegal in most nations today.

Cyber pornography covers pornographic websites, pornographic magazines produced using computers (to publish and print the material) and the Internet (to download and transmit pornographic pictures, photos, writings etc).

Section 67: Punishment for publishing or transmitting obscene material in electronic form (Amended vide ITAA 2008)

Whoever publishes or transmits or causes to be published or transmitted in the electronic form any material which contains sexually explicit act or conduct shall be punished on first conviction with imprisonment of either description for a term which may extend to five years and with fine which may extend to ten lakh rupees and in the event of second or subsequent conviction with imprisonment of either description for a term which may extend to seven years and also with fine which may extend to ten lakh rupees.

The Indian Penal Code, 1860 section 293 also specifies, in clear terms, the law against Sale etc. of obscene objects to minors. As per the IPC Act, 1860, Section 292- For the purposes of sub-section (2), a book, pamphlet, paper, writing, drawing, painting representation, figure or any other object, shall be deemed to be obscene if it is lascivious or appeals to the prurient interest or if its effect, or (where it comprises two or more distinct items) the effect of any one of its items, is, if taken as a whole, such as to tend to deprave and corrupt persons who are likely, having regard to all relevant circumstances, to read, see or hear the matter contained or embodied in it shall be punished with imprisonment, for the first instance, of either description for a term which may extend to two years, and with fine which may extend to two thousand rupees, and, in the event of a second or subsequent conviction, with imprisonment of either description for a term which may extend to five years, and also with fine which may extend to five thousand rupees.

Illustration 1

In the first case of this kind, the Delhi Police Cyber Crime Cell registered a case under section 67 of the IT Act, 2000. A student of the Air Force Balbharati School, New Delhi, was teased by all his classmates for having a pockmarked face, used a free hosting provider to create www.amazing-gents.8m.net.

He regularly uploaded "morphed" photographs of teachers and girls from his school onto the website. He was arrested when the father of one of the victims reported the case to the police.

Illustration 2

The CEO of online auction website bazee.com (a part of the

eBay group) was arrested by the Delhi police for violating India's strict laws on cyber pornography.

An engineering student was using the bazee website to sell a video depicting two school students having sexual intercourse. Bazee.com was held liable for distributing porn and hence the CEO was arrested.

Illustration 3

The CEO of a software company in Pune (India) was arrested for sending highly obscene emails to a former employee.

Child pornography: The newly inserted section 67B of IT Act Amendment, 2008 deals with child pornography. The wordings of the section are very hard worded and makes even the recording in electronic form of any sexually explicit act with children shall be punishable under this section. Even if one is found to be engaged in online relationship with sexual overtone that may offend a reasonable adult on the computer resource would be punishable under this section. The expression "May offend a reasonable adult" is subject to judicial scrutiny and interpretation and leaves scope for misuse and controversy.

Section 67B: Punishment for publishing or transmitting of material depicting children in sexually explicit act, etc. in electronic form. Whoever, -

a) Publishes or transmits or causes to be published or transmitted material in any electronic form which depicts children engaged in sexually explicit act or conduct or

b) creates text or digital images, collects, seeks, browses, downloads, advertises, promotes, exchanges or distributes material in any electronic form depicting children in obscene or indecent or sexually explicit manner or

c) cultivates, entices or induces children to online relationship with one or more children for and on sexually explicit act or in a manner that may offend a reasonable adult on the computer resource or

d) facilitates abusing children online or

e) records in any electronic form own abuse or that of others pertaining to sexually explicit act with children, shall be punished on first conviction with imprisonment of either description for a term which may extend to five years and with a fine which may extend to ten lakh rupees and in the event of second or subsequent conviction with imprisonment of either description for a term which may extend to seven years and also with fine which may extend to ten lakh rupees:

Provided that the provisions of section 67, section 67A and this section does not extend to any book, pamphlet, paper, writing, drawing, painting, representation or figure in electronic form

i. The publication of which is proved to be justified as being for the public good on the ground that such book, pamphlet, paper writing, drawing, painting, representation or figure is in the interest of science, literature, art or learning or other objects of general concern; or

ii. which is kept or used for bonafide heritage or religious purposes

Explanation: For the purposes of this section, "children" means a person who has not completed the age of 18 years.

Section 293: Sale, etc. of obscene objects to young persons – Whoever sells, lets to hire, distributes, exhibits or circulates to any person under the age of twenty years any such obscene object, as is referred to in IPC Section 292, or offers of attempts so to do, shall be punished (on first conviction with imprisonment or either description for a term which may extend to three years, and which fine which may extend to two thousand rupees, and, in the event of a second or subsequent conviction, with imprisonment of either description for a term which may extend to seven years, and also with fine which may extend to five thousand rupees)

CASE OF CHENNAI: The cybercrime police arrested Will Heum (Wilhelmus Weijdeveld) (56), a Dutch national living in Chennai, for uploading child pornographic materials on the internet. Police recovered his personal computer and pornographic materials from his house.

Heum is already facing a case in a Chengalpattu court for sexually abusing children of Little Home, an orphanage he had opened near Mamallapuram. He was arrested in May 2002. Out on bail and living in a rented house in Choolaimedu, he was uploading pictures of children being sexually abused, police said.

This is the **first case of child pornography** to be registered in the country under the IT Act, which came into force on October 27. Heum was booked under Section 67-B of the IT Act, 2008, which deals with digital child pornography, and remanded in judicial custody after being produced before the XI metropolitan magistrate court in Saidapet. The IT Act spells out a maximum punishment of seven years' imprisonment and a fine of Rs 10 lakh.

It was a tip-off from the Child Exploitation Online Protection Centre in Germany through Interpol that led to the arrest of Heum, who has done bit roles in Tamil movies.

Initial inquiries revealed that he had uploaded video clips of foreign children. "We are interrogating him about the source of these clips. We have to verify the seized computer accessories to check if he had uploaded clips of Indian children too," a police officer said.

"It was an example of good co-ordination between the city police and the international agencies. Cybercrime has no geographical barriers,"

Section 292, 293, 294 IPC, Indecent Representation of Women Act

Section 292: Sale, etc., or obscene books, etc.

(1) For the purposes of sub-section

(2), a book, pamphlet, paper, writing, drawing, painting, representation, figure or any other object, shall be deemed to be obscene if it is lascivious or appeals to the prurient interest or if its effect, or (where it comprises two or more distinct items) the effect of any one of its items, is, if taken as a whole, such as to tend to deprave and corrupt persons who are likely, having regard to all relevant circumstances, to read, see or hear the matter contained or embodied in it.

3(2) Whoever-

(a) Sells, lets to hire, distributes, publicly exhibits or in any manner puts into circulation, or for purposes of sale, hire, distribution, public exhibition or circulation, makes, produces or has in his possession any obscene book, pamphlet, paper, drawing, painting, representation or figure or any other obscene object whatsoever, or

(b) Imports, exports or conveys any obscene object for any of the purposes aforesaid, or knowing or having reason to believe that such object will be sold, let to hire, distributed or publicly exhibited or in any manner put into circulation, or

(c) Takes part in or receives profits from any business in the course of which he knows or has reason to believe that any such obscene objects are, for any of the purposes aforesaid, made, produced, purchased, kept, imported, exported, conveyed, publicly exhibited or in any manner put into circulation, or

(d) Advertises or makes known by any means whatsoever that any person is engaged or is ready to engage in any act which is an offence under this section, or that any such obscene object can be procured from or through any person, or

(e) Offers or attempts to do any act which is an offence under this section,

Shall be punished [on first conviction with imprisonment of either description for a term which may extend to two years, and with fine which may extend to two thousand rupees, and, in the event of a second or subsequent conviction, with imprisonment of either description for a term which may extend to five years, and also with fine which may extend to five thousand rupees].

Exception-This section does not extend to -

(a) Any book, pamphlet, paper, writing, drawing, painting, representation or figure-

(i) The publication of which is proved to be justified as being for the public good on the ground that such book, pamphlet, paper, writing, drawing, painting, representation or figure is in the interest of science, literature, art of learning or other objects of general concern, or

(ii) Which is kept or used bonafide for religious purposes;

(b) Any representation sculptured, engraved, painted or otherwise represented on or in-

(i) Any ancient monument within the meaning or the Ancient Monuments and Archaeological Sites and Remains Act, 1958 (24 of 1958), or

(ii) Any temple, or on any car used for the conveyance of idols, or kept or used for any religious purpose.

Section 292A: Printing etc. of grossly indecent or scurrilous matter or matter intended for blackmail

Whoever, -

(a) Prints or causes to be printed in any newspaper, periodical or circular, or exhibits or causes to be exhibited, to public view or distributes or causes to be distributed or in any manner puts into circulation any picture or any printed or written document which is grossly indecent, or in scurrilous or intended for blackmail, or

(b) Sells or lets for hire, or for purposes of sale or hire makes, produces or has in his possession, any picture or any printed or

written document which is grossly indecent or is scurrilous or intended for blackmail; or

(c) Conveys any picture or any printed or written document which is grossly indecent or is scurrilous or intended for blackmail knowing or having reason to believe that such picture or document will be printed, sold, let for hire distributed or publicly exhibited or in any manner put into circulation; or

(d) takes part in, or receives profits from, any business in the course of which he knows or has reason to believe that any such newspaper, periodical, circular, picture or other printed or written document is printed, exhibited, distributed, circulated, sold, let for hire, made, produced, kept, conveyed or purchased; or

(e) Advertises or makes known by any means whatsoever that any person is engaged or is ready to engage in any Act which is an offence under this section, or that any such newspaper, periodical, circular, picture or other printed or written document which is grossly indecent or is scurrilous or intended for blackmail, can be procured from or through any person; or

(f) Offers or attempts to do any act which is an offence under this section [shall be punished with imprisonment of either description for a term which may extend to two years, or with fine, or with both]:

Provided that for a second or any subsequent offence under this section, he shall be punished with imprisonment of either description for a term which shall not be less than six months and not more than two years.

Explanation I

For the purposes of this section, the word scurrilous shall be deemed to include any matter which is likely to be injurious to morality or is calculated to injure any person:

Provided that it is not scurrilous to express in good faith anything whatever respecting the conduct of-

(i) A public servant in the discharge of his public functions or respecting his character, so far as his character appears in that conduct and no further; or

(ii) Any person touching any public question, and respecting his character, so far as his character appears in that conduct and no further.

Explanation II

In deciding whether any person has committed an offence under this section, the Court shall have regard inter alia, to the following considerations-

(a) The general character of the person charged, and where relevant the nature of his business;

(b) The general character and dominant effect of the matter alleged to be grossly indecent or scurrilous or intended for blackmail;

(c) Any evidence offered or called by or on behalf of the accused person as to his intention in committing any of the acts specified in this section.

Section 293: Sale, etc., of obscene objects to young person

Whoever sells, lets to hire, distributes, exhibits or circulates

to any person under the age of twenty years any such obscene object as is referred to in the last preceding section, or offers or attempts so to do, shall be punished [on first conviction with imprisonment of either description for a term which may extend to three years, and with fine which may extend to two thousand rupees, and, in the event of a second or subsequent conviction, with imprisonment of either description for a term which may extend to seven years, and also with fine which may extend to five thousand rupees.

Section 294: Obscene acts and songs

Whoever, to the annoyance of others-

(a) Does any obscene act in any public place, or

(b) Sings, recites or utters any obscene song, balled or words, in or near any public place, shall be punished with imprisonment of either description for a term which may extend to three months, or with fine, or with both.

IPC Section 500: Punishment for defamation

Whoever defames another shall be punished with simple imprisonment for a term which may extend to two years, or with fine, or with both.

Clssification of Offence:

- Punishment – Simple imprisonment for 2 years, or fine, or both – Non-cognizable – bailable – triable by Court of Session – Compoundable by the person defamed.
- Punishment – Simple imprisonment for 2 years, or fine, or both – Non-cognizble – Bailable – Triable by Magistrate

of the first class – Compoundable by the person defamed with the permission of the court.

IPC Section 506: Punishment for criminal intimidation

Whoever commits, the offence of criminal intimidation shall be punished with imprisonment of either description for a term which may extend to two years, or with fine, or with both;

If threat be to cause death or grievous hurt, etc. –

And if the threat be to cause death or grievous hurt, or to cause the destruction of any property by fire, or to cause an offence punishable with death or [imprisonment for life], or with imprisonment for a term which may extend to seven years, or to impute, unchastity to a woman, shall be punished with imprisonment of either description for a term which may extend to seven years, or with fine, or with both.

Classification of offence

- Punishment – Imprisonment for 2 years, or fine, or both – Non-cognizable-Bailable - Triable by any Magistrate-Compundable by the person intimidated.
- Punishment – Imprisonment for 7 years, or fine, or both – Non-cognizable – Bailable – Triable by Magistrate of the first class – Non-compoundable.

IPC Section 509: Word, gesture, or act intended to insult the modesty of a woman

Whoever, intending to insult the modesty of any woman, utters any word, makes any sound or gesture, or exhibits any object, intending that such word or sound shall be heard, of that such gesture or object shall be seen, by such woman, or intrudes upon the privacy of such woman, [shall be punished with simple imprisonment for a term which may extend to three years, and also with fine.]

Classification of Offence:

Punishment - Simple imprisonment for 1 year, or fine, or both - Cognizable – Bailable - Triable by any Magistrate - Compoundable by the woman whom it was intended to insult or whose privacy was intruded upon with the permission of the court.

Cyber Bullying

With today's technology bullying has become easier that even the children and youth of this generation do not even need to have personal confrontation. Cyber bullying can be defined as any communication posted or sent by a minor online, by instant messenger, e-mail, Social Networking Site, website, diary site, online profile, interactive game, handheld device, cell phone or other interactive device that is intended to frighten, embarrass, harass or otherwise target another minor.

Cyber bullying is disturbingly common among Indian teens. Cyber-Bullying: Our Kids' New Reality is a survey that was conducted from December 2006 – January 2007 by the members of Kids Help Phone that had over 2500 respondents. More than 70 per cent of respondents to the survey reported that they have been bullied online, while 44 per cent said they have bullied someone online. At least 38% reported having experienced cyber-bullying within the last three months. Of the methods used, 77% reported being bullied by instant messaging, 37% by e-mail and 31% social networking sites, such as MySpace and Facebook. When bullied online, 43% said they did nothing, 32% confronted the person who bullied them, and 27% told a friend. Although most cyber bullying cases go unreported, police departments take action in trying to prevent it. Because many people are afraid to come to the police about an online problem, the police go to great lengths to find the problems themselves online.

A large number of youth and their parents think that cyber bullying is not a big enough deal to cause problems. However, it has been proven that a victim of this type of bullying may lead to serious disorders for the future including suicide.

When one becomes a victim of cyber bullying, they are a victim for life. Though the bullying itself may go away, the fear, the hurt, and the memories scar the victim forever.

Beat that bully:

The cyber bully is on the rise. Any type of bullying falls under the dominion of unpleasant and the cyber forum doesn't make it any different. Cyber bullying includes stalking, sending messages of a threatening nature, altering images and distributing them on the internet with the intentions of harassing or intimidating people. Don't respond to nasty messages. With the mobile phones and social networking sites ruling our lives, some immature individuals post nasty comments, send berating SMS messages and share humiliating pictures of videos.

Before you post something on the internet, pause for a minute and think over the contents. While sharing anything personal, be very conscious. Even if you know most of the people on your friend list personally, the information can be misused. It could be copied and made public, and once it's on the internet, it's very difficult to remove it later on. It pays to be courteous online. Manners never hurt anyone and this is the same in the online forum. This starts by treating people like the way you would like to be treated. Being mean can only attract troubles and bigger bullies picking on you.

In case you come across unflattering statements or statements on the internet that makes you uncomfortable, just ignore it or better, block the sender from your list. Most bullies are encouraged by retaliation and the situation would only get worse thereon. If you are being subjected to unwanted, abusive message, report this to an adult who you trust – your parents or a teacher. They would inform the service provider of the email or phone service and the bully can be taken to task. This will mean that the person who you confide in should take a broader perspective and take action immediately. If things still continue, inform the cybercrime division in your city. They would immediately get working on the culprit.

Before you approach the authorities, ensure that you have enough evidence. Save the messages or conversation thread on your social networking site. Again, get your parents or another adult into the picture. If this gets serious, approach the police.

If you see another person fall a victim to this behaviour, don't just watch. Encourage your friend or the person bullied to take action. Stand up for the victim. You can enlist your parent's help or even discuss this with your teacher. They would be able to take a call on this and safeguard you in case the issue turns vicious.

While the internet is a wonderful device and has become an imperceptible part of our lives, there's a lot out there that could cause serious trouble. The flip side is cybercrime and sadly, it is on the rise. The best thing to do is to be prepared. Follow these simple rules. Use your common sense and act smart. Think before you act and while conducting any online transactions, keep a wary eye. Being aware can help you stay away from cybercrime. After all, the internet can be full of good experiences if you take preventive measures and keep cyber criminals at bay with your resourcefulness.

Section 77B: Offences with three year's imprisonment to be cognizable

Notwithstanding anything contained in Criminal Procedure Code 1973, the offense punishable with imprisonment of three years and above shall be cognizable and the offence punishable with imprisonment of three years shall be bailable.

IPC Section 500: Punishment for defamation

Whoever defames another shall be punished with simple imprisonment for a term which may extend to two years, or with fine, or with both.

IPC Section 506: Punishment for criminal intimidation

Whoever commits, the offense of criminal intimidation shall be punished with imprisonment of either description for a term which may extend to two years, or with fine, or with both.

IPC Section 507: Criminal intimidation by an anonymous communication

Whoever commits the offence of criminal intimidation by an anonymous communication, or having taken precaution to conceal the name or abode of the person from whom the threat comes, shall be punished with imprisonment of either for a term which may extend to two years, in addition to the punishment provided for the offence by the last preceding section.

Illustration 1:

David Knight was oblivious to a website created all about him. For months, there had been a website that made fun of David and his family. They said things along the lines of that he was paedophile, he's gay and dirty. The website invited others to actively be involved with bashing this boy. Along with the website people were sending hateful emails telling him how much they don't like him. Thankfully, David did not physically harm himself like others you will read about.

Illustration 2:

When some girls stole Amanda Marcuson's belongings, she reported it. Later that night, she received instant messages calling her harsh names and saying she was a tattletale. Trying to defend herself, she replied that they had stolen her stuff and that just made it worse. When going out with her family, her internet messages were forwarded to her phone and she had received the maximum limit, 50, which were all threatening, intensely mean messages. The girls never even said another word to her, in person.

Illustration 3:

Jodi Plumb was distraught when she found out there was a website containing terrible comments about her. It was talking about her weight and they estimated a time of her death. Jodi's mom went straight to the school board and asked for harsher action taken about the bullies. Jodi had been attacked twice in school as well as people taking pictures of her for the website. Her mother was very upset.

Illustration 4:

An autistic thirteen-year-old that's sweet as can be just trying to make it through the days became a prime target of cyber bullying. Going through his days, and like any boy, he had that one crush. This girl that he had his eye on had stuck up for him for a while but soon became the main bully. She pretended to like him and then made fun of him and said, she would never like a guy like him. As his pain got worse, he had pen pal that was encouraging him to end his life. Ryan became so hurt he hung himself and all because of cyber bullies.

Identity Theft

Identity theft isn't a new criminal activity; in fact, it's been around for years. What's new is the method criminals are using to part people from their sensitive information. Fraud techniques have evolved at the same pace as technology developments.

Identity theft is a term used to refer to fraud that involves stealing money or getting other benefits by pretending to be someone else. The term is relatively new and is actually a misnomer, since it is not inherently possible to steal an identity, only to use it. The person whose identity is used can suffer various consequences when they are held responsible for the perpetrator's actions. At one time the only way for someone to steal somebody else's identity was by killing that person and taking his place. It was typically a violent crime. However, since then, the crime has evolved and today's white collared criminals are a lot less brutal. But the ramifications of an identity theft are still scary.

Identity theft occurs when someone steals your identity and pretends to be you to access resources such as credit cards, bank accounts and other benefits in your name. The imposter may also use your identity to commit other crimes.

As per the non-profit Identity Theft Resource Center, identity thefts can be sub-divided into four categories. These are financial identity theft, criminal identity theft, identity cloning, and business/commercial identity theft.

In many cases the victim is not even aware of what is being done till it is already too late. Identity theft may be used to facilitate crimes, including illegal immigration, terrorism, and espionage. It may also be used as a means of blackmail. There have also been cases of identity cloning to attack payment systems, including online credit card processing and medical insurance.

Sometimes people may impersonate others for non-financial reasons too. This is often done to receive praise or attention for the victim's achievements. This is sometimes referred to as identity theft in the media, and is a common trend seen by look-a-likes.

One does not have to think too far back before re-collecting a probable victim of identity theft in India.

Same Old Con Man, New Ride:

Con men and women have been around since the beginning of human history, and the computer and Internet just represent new tools for their scams. In this category fall the infamous Nigerian scammers, crooks, who trick you into unauthorized bank transfers and perform other forms of fraud. The difference between this and other types of cybercrime is that the crooks form a sort of relationship with the victim, fooling them into parting with their money. The bottom line with all the different types of cybercrime is that it's theft – of your personal information, your money and your trust – all things that ultimately make part of your identity. Although a lot of theft is more data theft than identity theft, it's difficult to draw a line because even if the crook is just stealing passwords, those passwords relate to your identity in some way. And once they get your username and password, it opens the door to getting a lot more data. Identity theft is one way to think about it, but you need to be on the guard for any kind of attack.

Illustration 1

An American national named Ken Haywood, whose most likely fault is, that his Wi-Fi internet connection was hacked, was only recently under the scanner for involvement in the Ahmadabad terrorist attacks. The sad part remains, while speculators and the cybercrime unit suspect foul play and hacking, not once has the term identity theft or identity protection been suggested.

And, this just goes to show our current level of awareness towards a threat so obvious.

Illustration 2

The biggest case of identity theft ever seen, took place in August of 2009. Eleven people, including a US secret service informant, had been charged in connection with the hacking of nine major retailers and the theft and sale of more than 41 million credit and debit card numbers! This data breach is believed to be the largest hacking and identity theft case ever prosecuted by the US Department of Justice, which announced that the suspects were charged with conspiracy, computer intrusion, fraud and identity theft. Three of those charged are US citizens, while the others are from places such as Estonia, Ukraine, Belarus and China.

The areas of data protection and securitisation are still very weak. How else could 11 people whose nations barely get along, pull of a heist involving a whooping 41 million credit card and debit card numbers. Yes, one can argue that this happened half-way across the globe and India is so much safer. But is it really? Forget the Ken Haywood incident; one might pass it off as an extreme case still in the grey area. But, when there was a duplicate Axis bank web page created, which was "phishing" for unsuspecting baits on the internet, the victims and crime was a lot closer home.

Illustration 3

Kingfisher Airlines was duped of Rs. 17 crore caused by an online ticket booking fraud, caused by credit card bookings. These credit card details were obtained by the thieves from various places like shopping mall, restaurant and petrol-pump employees who swipe these cards, felt the officers working on this case.

"Data loss is a burning issue that should be on the mind of every C-level executive and board member - if it isn't already. Every day we read about companies suffering millions of dollars in losses due to security breaches. Those losses directly hurt the innocent stakeholders of those companies, including hardworking employees and shareholders. Opportunity for data loss is everywhere, and intentional or otherwise, data that ends up in the wrong place can do tremendous harm. It might be at the hands of a single disgruntled employee with a flash drive, or a forgetful member of your finance department leaving a CD-ROM on the subway. But however it happens, data loss can be devastating, and it's only a matter of time before a high-profile company, perhaps a squeaky clean one bursting with integrity and good will, is brought to its knees by a breach" feels Dave DeWalt, McAfee, president and CEO, in McAfee's and Data monitor's latest research report.

Section 66C: Punishment for identity theft

Whoever, fraudulently or dishonestly make use of the electronic signature, password or any other unique identification feature of any other person, shall be punished with imprisonment of either description for a term which may extend to three years and shall also be liable to fine which may extend to rupees one lakh.

Section 66D: Punishment for cheating by personation by using computer resource

Whoever, by means of any communication device or computer resource cheats by personation, shall be punished with imprisonment of either description for a term which may extend to three years and shall also be liable to fine which may extend to one lakh rupees.

IPC Section 417A, that prescribes punishment of up to 3 years imprisonment and a fine for cheating, by using any unique identification feature of any other person.

IPC Section 419A, which prescribes punishment of up to 5 years imprisonment and a fine for cheating by impersonation, using a network or computer resource.

Sale of Illegal Articles on Internet

It is becoming increasingly common to find cases where sale of illegal articles such as narcotics drugs, weapons, wildlife etc. is being facilitated by the Internet.

Information about the availability of the products for sale is being posted on auction websites, bulletin boards etc.

It is practically impossible to control or prevent a criminal from setting up a website to transact in illegal articles. Additionally, there are several online payment gateways that can transfer money around the world at the click of a button.

The Internet has also created a marketplace for the sale of unapproved drugs, prescription drugs dispensed without a valid prescription, or products marketed with fraudulent health claims.

Many sites focus on selling prescription drugs and are referred to by some as "Internet pharmacies." These sites offer for sale either approved prescription drug products, or in some cases, unapproved, illegal versions of prescription drugs. This poses a serious potential threat to the health and safety of patients. The broad reach, relative anonymity, and ease of creating new or removing old websites, poses great challenges for law enforcement officials.

As pointed out earlier, the online lottery is the most popular form of internet gambling in India. Most companies marketing and distributing or conducting state government-sponsored lotteries through the internet are not allowed to sell their services in the states that banned lotteries. In most cases, these marketers and distributors limit their online services to consumers who are residents of the states where a lottery is permissible. Notwithstanding the fact there has been no reported case of breach by any company promoting online lotteries, most of these companies (as a safeguard) seek an undertaking from their consumers relating to their residence.

There have been instances where one state has banned the lottery of other states, including online lotteries. In a recent case, the Karnataka High Court upheld the decision of the Karnataka government to make itself a 'lottery free zone' by imposing a ban on lotteries of all other states, including online lotteries under the Lotteries (Regulation) Act 1998. The state government, in this case, directed the closure of the terminals and kiosks selling the online lotteries.

Enforcement over foreign jurisdictions

If the websites were hosted and operated from outside India, it was difficult for the Indian authorities to issue any directive to close them down or prohibit their access without using its blocking powers under the ITA but under ITA 2008. The authorities have little to worry about, as Indian foreign exchange laws do not permit remittances outside India for gambling related activity, such as the purchase of lottery tickets, football pools and sweepstakes. As a result, a gambling website hosted outside India aiming at receiving money from within India cannot do so through legal channels.

Illustration

Many of the auction sites even in India are believed to be selling cocaine in the name of 'honey'. The clip of the DPS students was kept for selling on the site called Bazee.com by a student from IIT Kharagpur.

Case filed under - NDPS Act

Illustration

In March 2007, the Pune rural police cracked down on an illegal rave party and arrested hundreds of illegal drug users. The social networking site Orkut.com is believed to be one of the modes of communication for gathering people for the illegal "drug" party.

Case is filed under - NDPS Act

Online sale of Arms - **Arms Act will be applicable**

Illustration 1:

The Supreme Court deciding a special leave petition touched on Section 79 of the Information Technology Act, 2000. The Petitioner (Sanjay Kumar Kedia) was ostensibly running an online pharmacy which was allegedly used to sell psychotropic substances to customers without prescriptions. He was subsequently issued a notice Section 67 of the Narcotic Drugs and Psychotropic Substances Act, 1985. Thereafter the petitioner filed an application for bail several times which was rejected by the courts and hence preferred the special leave petition to appeal against the orders for refusal of bail. The counsel for the petitioner cited section 79 as a defense stating that it granted immunity from prosecution. He stated that the companies of the petitioner only provided third party data and information without any knowledge as to the commission of an offence under the Act. The respondents (Narcotics Control Bureau) rebutted this by stating that the petitioner and its associates are not an intermediary as defined under section 79 of the said Act as their acts and deeds was not simply restricted to provision of third party data or information without having knowledge as to commission of offence under the NDPS Act. The company (Xponse Technologies Ltd. And Xpose IT Services Pvt. Ltd headed by Sanjay Kedia) has designed, developed, hosted the pharmaceutical websites and was using these websites, huge quantity of psychotropic substances (Phentermine and Butalbital) have been distributed in USA with the help of his associates. The Supreme Court quite correctly applying the law as it stands held that (a) the petitioner was not an innocent intermediary as defined under section 79 of the Technology Act according to the investigating agencies, they were the owners and were responsible for the contents therein; and (b) Section 79 will grant immunity to an accused who has violated the provisions of the Information Technology Act, 2000 and not grant an immunity under the Narcotic Drugs and Psychotropic Substances Act, 1985.

Online Gambling

There are thousands of Websites that offer Online Gambling. The special issue with online gambling is that it is legalised in several countries. So legally the owners of these websites are safe in their home countries. Virtual casinos, Cases of money laundering etc. are online cases.

The legal issues arise when a person residing in a foreign country like India (where such website are illegal) gambles on such a website.

The law related to gambling is also applicable to online gambling. All gambling contracts are considered to be wagering contracts and it is not possible to enforce such contracts under the ICA, detailed below.

Illustration

The website ladbrokes.com permits users to gamble on a variety of sports such as cricket, football, tennis, golf, motor racing, ice hockey, basketball, baseball, darts, snooker, boxing, athletics', rugby, volleyball, motor cycling etc.

Additionally it also features an online casino. The website has no technical measures in place to prohibit residents of certain countries (where online gambling is illegal) from betting at their website.

Cyber lotto case: In Andhra Pradesh one Kola Mohan created a website and an email address on the Internet with the address 'eurolottery@usa.net' which shows his own name as beneficiary of 12.5 million pound in Euro lottery. After getting confirmation with the email address a Telugu newspaper published this as news.

He gathered huge sums from the public as well as from some banks. The fraud came to light only when a cheque amounting Rs 1.73 million discounted by him with Andhra bank got dishonoured.

The law relating to online gambling in India needs to be understood within the country's socio-cultural context. At the outset, gambling, although not absolutely prohibited in India, does not receive express encouragement by policy makers. The Indian organized gambling industry is estimated to be worth around US$8 billion. While stringent laws have checked the proliferation of casinos and high street gaming centres as in many other countries, barring the state of Goa, the lottery business remains the most post popular form of gambling.

Though gambling is not illegal, it is a highly controlled and regulated activity. Modern India is a quasi-federal Constitutional democracy and the powers to legislate are distributed at the federal as well as the state levels. Gambling features in List II of the Constitution of India, this implies that the state governments have the authority to enact laws in order to regulate gambling in the respective states. Thus, there is no single law governing gambling in the entire country. Different states have different laws governing gambling in addition to the laws that have an application across the country. While some states have banned lotteries, other states allow state government lotteries marketed and distributed in other lottery playing and promoting states through private entities.

Regulation of gambling

The courts have defined gambling as 'the payment of a price for a chance to win a prize'. The dominant element of skill or chance shall determine the nature of the game. A game may be deemed to be gambling if the element of chance or luck predominates in deciding its outcome. As a result, Indian courts have held that betting on horse racing and a few card games are not gambling. The right to undertake the business of gambling and lotteries is not considered as a fundamental right protected by the Constitution of India. It may however be pointed out that the state government run lotteries make significant contributions to the state exchequer of several state governments and the Union government, and hence there is a resistance to complete prohibition.

The following legislation is pertinent to gambling:

The Public Gaming Act, 1867

This Act provides punishment for public gambling and for keeping of a 'common gaming house'. This Act also authorises the state governments to enact laws to regulate public gambling in their respective jurisdictions. The penal legislations in respective states have been amended in accordance with their policy on gambling. However, this legislation does not have any direct impact on online gambling unless a wide interpretation is given to the definition of common gaming house so as to include virtual forums as well.

The Indian Contract Act, 1872 (ICA)

The ICA is a codified umbrella legislation that governs all commercial contracts in India. Under the ICA, a wagering contract is the one which cannot be enforced.

The Act lays down; 'Agreements by way of wager are void, and no suit shall be brought for recovering anything alleged to be won on any wager or entrusted to any person to abide by the result of any game or other uncertain event on which any wager is made'. Gambling, lottery and prize games have held to be wagering contracts and thus void and unenforceable. While a wagering contract is not illegal, it cannot be enforced in a court of law. Thus, the courts will not entertain any cause of action that arises out of a wagering contract.

Lotteries (Regulation) Act, 1998

This Act provides a framework for organizing lotteries in the country. Under this Act, the state governments have been authorized to promote as well as prohibit lotteries within their territorial jurisdiction. This Act also provides for the manner in which the lotteries are to be conducted and prescribes punishment in case of breach of its provision. Lotteries not authorized by the state have been made an offence under the Indian Penal Code. Several non-lottery playing states, like Gujarat and Uttar Pradesh, have prohibited the sale of other state-government lotteries under this Act.

Indian Penal Code, 1860

Section 294A: deals with keeping lottery office. It says that whoever keeps any office or place for the purpose of drawing any lottery not being a State lottery or a lottery authorised by the State Government, shall be punished with imprisonment of either description for a term which may extend to six months, or with fine, or with both.

And whoever publishes any proposal to pay any sum, or to deliver any goods, or to do or forbear doing anything for the benefit of any person, on any event or contingency relative or applicable to the drawing of any ticket, lot, number or figure in any such lottery, shall be punished with fine which may extend to one thousand rupees.

Illustration 1

Recent Indian case about cyber lotto was very interesting. A man called Kola Mohan invented the story of winning the Euro Lottery. He himself created a website and an email address on the Internet with the address 'eurolottery@usa.net'. Whenever accessed, the site would name him as the beneficiary of the 12.5/- million. After confirmation a Telugu newspaper published this as news. He collected huge sums from the public as well as from some banks for mobilization of the deposits in foreign currency.

However, the fraud came to light when a cheque discounted by him with the Andhra Bank for Rs. 1.73/- million bounced. Mohan had pledged with Andhra Bank the copy of a bond certificate purportedly issued by Midland Bank, Sheffields, London, stating that a term deposit of Rs. 12.5/- million was held in his name.

Illustration 2

The website getwin.com permits users to gamble on a variety of sports such as cricket, football, tennis, golf, motor racing, ice hockey, basketball, baseball, darts, snooker, boxing, athletics, rugby, volleyball, motor cycling etc.

Additionally it also has links to online casino. The website has no technical measures in place to prohibit residents of India (where online gambling is illegal) from betting at their website. Indian citizens if caught gambling on this website would be booked under Indian laws.

Intellectual Property Crimes

These include software piracy, copyright infringement, trademarks violations, theft of computer source code etc.

Illustration 1

Bharti Cellular Ltd. filed a case in the Delhi High Court that some cyber squatters had registered domain names such as barticellular.com and bhartimobile.com with Network Solutions under different fictitious names. The court directed Network Solutions not to transfer the domain names in question to any third party and the matter is sub judice.

Illustration 2

Yahoo had sued one Akash Arora for use of the domain name 'Yahooindia.Com' deceptively similar to its 'Yahoo.com'. As this case was governed by the Trade Marks Act, 1958, the additional defence taken against Yahoo's legal action for the interim order was that the Trade Marks Act was applicable only to goods.

Illustration 3

A software professional from Bangalore (India) was booked for stealing the source code of a product being developed by his employers. He started his own company and allegedly used the stolen source code to launch a new software product.

Illustration 4

In 2003, a computer user in China obtained the source code of a popular game – Lineage II from an unprotected website. This proprietary code was then sold to several people in 2004. One of those people set up a website, www.l2extreme.com, to offer the "Lineage" game at a discount.

Despite legal warnings from the South Korean company that owned the Lineage source code, the suspect did not shut down the site. He rented powerful servers enough to accommodate 4,000 simultaneous gamers - and solicited donations from users to help defray the costs.

The loss in potential revenues for the South Korean company was estimated at $750,000 a month. The US FBI arrested the suspect and the website was shut down.

For Piracy - Section 51, 63, 63B Copyright Act will be applicable.

CHAPTER XI: INFRINGEMENT OF COPYRIGHT

When copyright infringed

Section 51: Copyright in a work shall be deemed to be infringed -

(a) when any person, without a licence granted by the owner of the copyright or the Registrar of Copyrights under this Act or in contravention of the conditions of a licence so granted or of any condition imposed by a competent authority under this Act-

(i) does anything, the exclusive right to do which is by this Act conferred upon the owner of the copyright; or

(ii) permits for profit any place to be used for the communication of the work to the public where such communication constitutes an infringement of the copyright in the work, unless he was not aware and had no reasonable ground for believing that such communication to the public would be an infringement of copyright; or

(b) when any person-

(i) makes for sale or hire, or sells or lets for hire, or by way of trade displays or offers for sale or hire, or

(ii) distributes either for the purpose of trade or to such an extent as to affect prejudicially the owner of the copyright, or

(iii) by way of trade exhibits in public, or

(iv) imports (except for the private and domestic use of the importer) into India, any infringing copies of the work.

Explanation - For the purposes of this section, the reproduction of a literary, dramatic, musical or artistic work in the form of a cinematograph film shall be deemed to be an "infringing copy".

Offence of infringement of copyright or other rights conferred by this Act

Section 63: Any person who knowingly infringes or abets the infringement of-

(a) the copyright in a work, or

(b) any other right conferred by this Act, except the right conferred by section 53A,

shall be punishable with imprisonment for a term which shall not be less than six months but which may extend to three years and with fine which shall not be less than fifty thousand rupees but which may extend to two lakh rupees:

PROVIDED that where the infringement has not been made for gain in the course of trade or business the court may, for adequate and special reasons to be mentioned in the judgment, impose a sentence of imprisonment for a term of less than six months or a fine of less than fifty thousand rupees.

Explanation: Construction of a building or other structure which infringes or which, if completed, would infringe the copyright in some other work shall not be an offence under this section.

Section 63A: Enhanced penalty on second and subsequent convictions.—Whoever having already been convicted of an offence under section 63 is again convicted of any such offence shall be punishable for the second and for every subsequent offence, with imprisonment for a term which shall not be less than one year but which may extend to three years and with fine which shall not be less than one lakh rupees but which may extend to two lakhs rupees:

PROVIDED that where the infringement has not been made for gain in the course of trade or business the court may, for adequate and special reasons to be mentioned in the judgment, impose a sentence of imprisonment for a term of less than one year or a fine of less than one lakh rupees: Provided further that for the purposes of this section, no cognizance shall be taken of any conviction made before the commencement of the Copyright (Amendment) Act, 1984 (65 of 1984).

Section 63B: Knowing use of infringing copy of computer programme to be an offence. - Any person who knowingly makes use on a computer of an infringing copy of a computer programme shall be punishable with imprisonment for a term which shall not be less than seven days but which may extend to three years and with fine which shall not be less than fifty thousand rupees but which may extend to two lakh rupees:

PROVIDED that where the computer programme has not been used for gain or in the course of trade or business, the court may, for adequate and special reasons to be mentioned in the judgment, not impose any sentence of imprisonment and may impose a fine which may extend to fifty thousand rupees.

IPC Section 405: Criminal breach of trust

Whoever, being in any manner entrusted with property, or with any dominion over property, dishonestly misappropriates or converts to his own use that property, or dishonestly uses or disposes of that property in violation of any direction of law prescribing the mode in which such trust is to be discharged, or of any legal contract, express or implied, which he has made touching the discharge of such trust, or willfully suffers any other person so to do, commits "criminal breach of trust".

IPC Section 420: Cheating and dishonestly inducing delivery of property

Whoever cheats and thereby dishonestly induces the person deceived any property to any person, or to make, alter or destroy the whole or any part of a valuable security, or anything which is signed or sealed, and which is capable of being converted into a valuable security, shall be punished with imprisonment of either description for a term which may extend to seven years, and shall also be liable to fine.

Classification of Offence:

Punishment - Imprisonment for 7 years and fine - Compoundable by the person cheated with the permission of the court.

IPC Section 120B: Punishment of Criminal Conspiracy

Whoever is a party to a criminal conspiracy to commit an offence punishable with death, 2[imprisonment for life] or rigorous imprisonment for a term of two years or upwards, shall, where no express provision is made in this Code for the punishment of such a conspiracy, be punished in the same manner as if he had abetted such offence.

(2) Whoever is a party to a criminal conspiracy other than a criminal conspiracy to commit an offence punishable as aforesaid shall be punished with imprisonment of either description for a term not exceeding six months, or with fine or with both.

IPC Section 468: Forgery for purpose of cheating

Whoever commits forgery, intending that the 1[document

or Electronic Record forged] shall be used for the purpose of cheating, shall be punished with imprisonment of either description for a term which may extend to seven years, and shall also be liable to fine.

Classification of Offence:

Punishment—Imprisonment for 7 years and fine—Cognizable—Non-bailable—-Triable by Magistrate of the first class—Non-compoundable

IPC Section 471: Using as genuine a forged document or electronic record

Whoever fraudulently or dishonestly uses as genuine any [document or electronic record] which he knows or has reason to believe to be a forged [document or electronic record], shall be punished in the same manner as if he had forged such [document or electronic record].

Classification of Offence:

Punishment - Punishment for forgery of such document – Cognizable – Bailable - Triable by Magistrate of the first class - Non-compoundable.

E-Mail Spoofing

A spoofed e-mail is one that appears to originate from one source but actually has been sent from another source e.g. Rama has an e-mail address rama@academiicarista.com. His ex-girlfriend, Pooja spoofs his e-mail and sends obscene messages to all his friends and colleagues. Since the e-mails appear to have originated from Rama, his friends may take offence and relationships may be spoiled for life.

Falsifying the name and / or email address of the originator of the email does e-mail spoofing usually to send an e-mail the sender has to enter the following information:

- e-mail address of the receiver of the e-mail
- e-mail address(es) of the person(s) who will receive a copy of the e-mail (referred to as CC for carbon copy)
- e-mail address(es) of the person(s) who will receive a copy of the e-mail (referred to as CC for carbon copy, but whose identities will not be known to the other recipients of the e-mail (known as BCC for blind carbon copy)
- Subject of the message (a short title / description of the message)
- Message

Certain web-based e-mail services like www.sendfakemail.com offer a facility wherein addition to the above, a sender can also enter the e-mail address of the purported sender of the e-mail.

E-mail spoofing is possible because the Simple Mail Transfer Protocol (SMTP) does not provide a mechanism for address authentication. Although e-mail address authentication protocols and mechanisms have been specified to battle e-mail spoofing, adoption of those mechanisms has been slow.

To prevent becoming a victim of email spoofing, be wary of tactics used in social engineering and contact the sender directly when sharing private or financial information instead of responding through an email.

Forgery of electronic records, E-mail Spoofing under IT Act Amendment 2008 Section 66A, 66C.

Section 66A: Punishment for sending offensive messages through communication service

Any person who sends, by means of a computer resource or a communication device,

a) any information that is grossly offensive or has menacing character; or

b) any information which he knows to be false, but for the purpose of causing annoyance, inconvenience, danger, obstruction, insult, injury, criminal intimidation, enmity, hatred, or ill will, persistently makes by making use of such computer resource or a communication device,

c) any electronic mail or electronic mail message for the purpose of causing annoyance or inconvenience or to deceive or to mislead the addressee or recipient about the origin of such messages shall be punishable with imprisonment for a term which may extend to two three years and with fine.

Explanation: For the purposes of this section, terms "Electronic Mail" and "Electronic Mail Message" means a message or information created or transmitted or received on a computer, computer system, computer resource or communication device including attachments in text, image, audio, video and any other electronic record, which may be transmitted with the message.

Section 66C: Punishment for identity theft

Whoever, fraudulently or dishonestly make use of the electronic signature, password or any other unique identification feature of any other person, shall be punished with imprisonment of either description for a term which may extend to three years and shall also be liable to fine which may extend to rupees one lakh.

Section 463, 464, 468, 469 IPC

Illustration 1

In an American case, a teenager made millions of dollars by spreading false information about certain companies whose shares he had short sold.

This misinformation was spread by sending spoofed emails, purportedly from news agencies like Reuters, to share brokers and investors who were informed that the companies were doing very badly.

Even after the truth came out the values of the shares did not go back to the earlier levels and thousands of investors lost a lot of money.

Illustration 2

A branch of the erstwhile Global Trust Bank in India experienced a run on the bank. Numerous customers decided to withdraw all their money and close their accounts.

An investigation revealed that someone had sent out spoofed emails to many of the bank's customers stating that the bank was in very bad shape financially and could close operations at any time. The spoofed email appeared to have originated from the bank itself. Unfortunately this information proved to be true in the next few days.

Case of Cyber Extortion and E-mail Spoofing

He does not know much about computer hacking, yet 51-year-old cybercriminal Pranab Mitra has stunned even the cybercrime investigation cell of Mumbai police with his bizarre fraud on the Net. Mitra, a former executive of Gujarat Ambuja Cement, was arrested in June 09 for posing as a woman and seducing online an Abu Dhabi-based man, thereby managing to extort Rs 96 lakh from him. Investigating officer he was remanded to police custody and has been booked for cheating, impersonation, blackmail and extortion under sections 384, 420, 465, 467, 471, 474 of the IPC, read with the newly formed Information Technology Act 2008 66D

Section 66D: Punishment for cheating by personation by using computer resource

Whoever, by means of any communication device or computer resource cheats by personation, shall be punished with imprisonment of either description for a term which may extend to three years and shall also be liable to fine which may extend to one lakh rupees.

Case Story:

Mitra posed as a woman, Rita Basu, and created a fake e-mail ID through which he contacted one V.R. Ninawe. According to the FIR, Mitra trapped Ninawe in a "cyber-relationship" sending emotional messages and indulging in online sex since June 2002. Later, Mitra sent an e-mail that "she would commit suicide" if Ninawe ended the relationship. He also gave him another friend Ruchira Sengupta's e-mail ID which was in fact his second bogus address. When Ninawe mailed at the other ID he was shocked to learn that Mitra had died. Then Mitra began the emotional blackmail by calling up Abu Dhabi to say that police here were searching for Ninawe. Ninawe panicked on hearing the news and asked Mitra to arrange for a good advocate for his defence. Ninawe even deposited a few lakh in the bank as advocate fees. Mitra even sent e-mails as high court and police officials to extort more money. Ninawe finally came down to Mumbai to lodge a police case.

Forgery

Counterfeit currency notes, postage and revenue stamps, mark sheets, academic certificates etc. are made by criminals using sophisticated computers, printers and scanners.

IPC Section 463: Forgery

Whoever makes any false documents or false electronic record or part of a document or electronic record, with intent to cause damage or injury, to the public or to any person, or to support any claim or title, or to cause any person to part with property, or to enter into any express or implied contract, or with intent to commit fraud or that fraud may be committed, commits forgery.

IPC Section 464: Making a false document

A person is said to make a false document or false electronic record-

First - Who dishonestly or fraudulently-

(a) Makes, signs, seals or executes a document or part of a document;

(b) Makes or transmits any electronic record or part of any electronic record;

(c) Affixes any digital signature on any electronic record;

(d) Makes any mark denoting the execution of a document or the authenticity of the digital signature,

With the intention of causing it to be believed that such document or part of document, electronic record or digital signature was made, signed, sealed, executed, transmitted or affixed by or by the authority of a person by whom or by whose authority he knows that it was not made, signed, sealed, executed or affixed; or

Secondly - Who, without lawful authority, dishonestly or fraudulently, by cancellation or otherwise, alters a document or an electronic record in any material part thereof, after it has been made, executed or affixed with digital signature either by himself or by any other person, whether such person be living or dead at the time of such alteration; or

Thirdly- Who dishonestly or fraudulently causes any person to sign, seal, execute or alter a document or an electronic record or to affix his digital signature on any electronic record knowing that such person by reason of unsoundness of mind or intoxication cannot, or that by reason of deception practiced upon him, he does not know the contents of the document or electronic record or the nature of the alteration.

Section 468: Forgery for purpose of cheating

Whoever commits forgery, intending that the [document or Electronic Record forged] shall be used for the purpose of cheating, shall be punished with imprisonment of either description for a term which may extend to seven years, and shall also be liable to fine.

Section 469: Forgery for purpose of harming reputation

Whoever commits forgery, [intending that the document or Electronic Record forged] shall harm the reputation of any party, or knowing that it is likely to used for that purpose, shall be punished with imprisonment of either description for a term which may extend to three years, and shall also be liable to fine.

IPC Section 470: Forged document or electronic record

A false [document or electronic record] made wholly or in part by forgery is designated "a forged [document or electronic record]".

IT Act 2008 Section 65: Tampering with Computer Source Documents

Whoever knowingly or intentionally conceals, destroys or alters or intentionally or knowingly causes another to conceal, destroy or alter any computer source code used for a computer, computer programme, computer system or computer network, when the computer source code is required to be kept or maintained by law for the time being in force, shall be punishable with imprisonment up to three years, or with fine which may extend up to two lakh rupees, or with both.

Explanation - For the purposes of this section, "Computer Source Code" means the listing of programmes.

Illustration 1

In October 1995, Economic Offences Wing of Crime Branch, Mumbai (India), seized over 22,000 counterfeit share certificates of eight reputed companies worth Rs. 34.47 crores.

These were allegedly prepared using Desktop Publishing Systems.

Illustration 2

Abdul Kareem Telgi, along with several others, was convicted in India on several counts of counterfeiting stamp papers and postage stamps totalling several billion rupees.

Cyber Defamation

This occurs when defamation takes place with the help of computers and / or the Internet. E.g. Rama publishes defamatory matter about Pooja on a website or sends e-mails containing defamatory information to Pooja's friends.

Section 66A: Punishment for sending offensive messages through communication service

Any person who sends, by means of a computer resource or a communication device,-

a) any information that is grossly offensive or has menacing character; or

b) any information which he knows to be false, but for the purpose of causing annoyance, inconvenience, danger, obstruction, insult, injury, criminal intimidation, enmity, hatred, or ill will, persistently makes by making use of such computer resource or a communication device,

c) any electronic mail or electronic mail message for the purpose of causing annoyance or inconvenience or to deceive or to mislead the addressee or recipient about the origin of such messages shall be punishable with imprisonment for a term which may extend to three years and with fine.

Explanation - For the purposes of this section, terms "Electronic Mail" and "Electronic Mail Message" means a message or information created or transmitted or received on a computer, computer system, computer resource or communication device including attachments in text, image, audio, video and any other electronic record, which may be transmitted with the message.

IPC Section 500: Punishment for defamation

Whoever defames another shall be punished with simple imprisonment for a term which may extend to two years, or with fine, or with both.

IPC Section 509: Word, gesture or act intended to insult the modesty of a woman

Whoever, intending to insult the modesty of any woman, utters any word, makes any sound or gesture, or exhibits any object, intending that such word or sound shall be heard, of that such gesture or object shall be seen, by such woman, or intrudes upon the privacy of such woman, shall be punished with simple imprisonment for a term which may extend to three years, and also with fine.

Classification of Offence

Punishment – Simple imprisonment for 1 year, or fine, or both – Compoundable by the woman whom it was intended to insult or whose privacy was intruded upon with the permission of the court.

Illustration 1

Abhishek, a teenaged student was arrested by the Thane police in India following a girl's complaint about tarnishing her image in the social networking site Orkut.

Abhishek had allegedly created a fake account in the name of the girl with her mobile number posted on the profile.

The profile had been sketched in such a way that it drew lewd comments from many who visited her profile. The Thane Cyber Cell tracked down Abhishek from the false e-mail id that he had created to open up the account.

Illustration 2

The Aurangabad bench of the Bombay high court issued a notice to Google.com following a public interest litigation initiated by a young lawyer.

The lawyer took exception to a community called 'We hate India', owned by someone who identified himself as Miroslav Stankovic. The community featured a picture of the Indian flag being burnt.

Illustration 3

Unidentified persons posted obscene photographs and contact details of a Delhi school girl. Suggestive names like 'sex teacher' were posted on the profile. The matter came to light after the girl's family started receiving vulgar calls referring to Orkut.

Cyber Stalking

Cyber stalking refers to the use of the Internet, e-mail, or other electronic communications devices to stalk another person.

Stalking generally involves harassing or threatening behaviour that an individual engages in repeatedly, such as following a person, appearing at a person's home or place of business, making harassing phone calls, leaving written messages or objects, or vandalizing a person's property.

Most stalking laws require that the perpetrator make a credible threat of violence against the victim; others include threats against the victim's immediate family.

IPC Section 503: Criminal intimidation:

Whoever threatens another with any injury to his person, reputation or property, or to the person or reputation of any one in whom that person is interested, with intent to cause alarm to that person, or to cause that person to do any act which he is not legally bound to do, or to omit to do any act which that person is legally entitled to do, as the means of avoiding the execution of such threat, commits criminal intimidation.

Explanation - A threat to injure the reputation of any deceased person in whom the person threatened is interested, is within this section.

2. **Sending defamatory messages by email**

IPC Section 499: Defamation

Whoever, by words either spoken or intended to be read, or by signs or by visible representations, makes or publishes any imputation concerning any person intending to harm, or knowing or having reason to believe that such imputation will harm, the reputation of such person, is said, except in the cases hereinafter expected, of defame that person.

Explanation 1

It may amount to defamation to impute anything to a deceased person, if the imputation would harm the reputation of that person if living, and is intended to be hurtful to the feelings of his family or other near relatives.

Explanation 2

It may amount to defamation to make an imputation concerning a company or an association or collection of persons as such.

Explanation 3

An imputation in the form of an alternative or expressed ironically, may amount to defamation.

Explanation 4

No imputation is said to harm a person's reputation, unless that imputation directly or indirectly, in the estimation of others, lowers the moral or intellectual character of that person, or lowers the character of that person in respect of his caste or of his calling, or lowers the credit of that person, or causes it to be believed that the body of that person is in a loathsome state, or in a state generally considered as disgraceful

Illustration 1

Ritu Kohli has the dubious distinction of being the first lady to register the cyber stalking case. A friend of her husband gave her telephonic number in the general chat room. The general chatting facility is provided by some websites like MIRC and ICQ where person can easily chat without disclosing his true identity. The friend of husband also encouraged this chatters to speak in slang language to Ms. Kohli.

IPS Section 509: Word, gesture or act intended to insult the modesty of a woman

Whoever, intending to insult the modesty of any woman, utters any word, makes any sound or gesture, or exhibits any object, intending that such word or sound shall be heard, of that such gesture or object shall be seen, by such woman, or intrudes upon the privacy of such woman, shall be punished with simple imprisonment for a term which may extend to three years, and also with fine.

Classification of Offence:

Punishment - Simple imprisonment for 1 year, or fine, or both. Compoundable by the woman whom it was intended to insult or whose privacy was intruded upon with the permission of the court.

IT Act 2008: Section 66A: Punishment for sending offensive messages through communication service

Any person who sends, by means of a computer resource or a communication device,-

a) Any information that is grossly offensive or has menacing character; or

b) any information which he knows to be false, but for the purpose of causing annoyance, inconvenience, danger, obstruction, insult, injury, criminal intimidation, enmity, hatred, or ill will, persistently makes by making use of such computer resource or a communication device,

c) any electronic mail or electronic mail message for the purpose of causing annoyance or inconvenience or to deceive or to mislead the addressee or recipient about the origin of such messages

shall be punishable with imprisonment for a term which may extend to three years and with fine.

Explanation: For the purposes of this section, terms "Electronic Mail" and "Electronic Mail Message" means a message or information created or transmitted or received on a computer, computer system, computer resource or communication device including attachments in text, image, audio, video and any other electronic record, which may be transmitted with the message.

Illustration 2

In the first successful prosecution under the California (USA) cyber stalking law, prosecutors obtained a guilty plea from a 50-year-old former security guard who used the Internet to solicit the rape of a woman who rejected his romantic advances. He terrorized the 28-year-old victim by impersonating her in various Internet chat rooms and online bulletin boards, where he posted, along with her telephone number and address, messages that she fantasized about being raped. On at least six occasions, sometimes in the middle of the night, men knocked on the woman's door saying they wanted to rape her.

Illustration 3

An honors graduate from the University of San Diego in USA terrorized five female university students over the Internet for more than a year. The victims received hundreds of violent and threatening e-mails, sometimes receiving four or five messages a day. The student, who pleaded guilty, told the police that he had committed the crimes because he thought the women were laughing at him and causing others to ridicule him. In reality, the victims had never met him.

Illustration 4

In 2005, a minor from Massachusetts (USA) was convicted in connection with approximately $1 million in victim damages. Over a 15-month period, he had hacked into Internet and telephone service providers, stolen an individual's personal information and posted it on the Internet, and made bomb threats to many high schools.

Web Defacement

Website defacement is usually the substitution of the original home page of a website with another page (usually pornographic or defamatory in nature) by a hacker.

Religious and government sites are regularly targeted by hackers in order to display political or religious beliefs. Disturbing images and offensive phrases might be displayed in the process, as well as a signature of sorts, to show who was responsible for the defacement.

Websites are not only defaced for political reasons, many defacers do it just for the thrill. For example, there are online contests in which hackers are awarded points for defacing the largest number of web sites in a specified amount of time. Corporations are also targeted more often than other sites on the Internet and they often seek to take measures to protect themselves from defacement or hacking in general.

Web sites represent the image of a company or organisation and these are therefore especially vulnerable to defacement. Visitors may lose faith in sites that cannot promise security and will become wary of performing online transactions. After defacement, sites have to be shut down for repairs, sometimes for an extended period of time, causing expenses and loss of profit.

IPC Section 463: Forgery

Whoever makes any false documents or electronic record part of a document or electronic record with, intent to cause damage or injury, to the public or to any person, or to support any claim or title, or to cause any person to part with property, or to enter into any express or implied contract, or with intent to commit fraud or that fraud may be committed, commits forgery.

IPC Section 464: Making a false document

A person is said to make a false document or false electronic record-

First-Who dishonestly or fraudulently-

(a) Makes, signs, seals or executes a document or part of a document;

(b) Makes or transmits any electronic record or part of any electronic record;

(c) Affixes any digital signature on any electronic record;

(d) Makes any mark denoting the execution of a document or the authenticity of the digital signature,

With the intention of causing it to be believed that such document or part of document, electronic record or digital signature was made, signed, sealed, executed, transmitted or affixed by or by the authority of a person by whom or by whose authority he knows that it was not made, signed, sealed, executed or affixed; or

Secondly - Who, without lawful authority, dishonestly or fraudulently, by cancellation or otherwise, alters a document or an electronic record in any material part thereof, after it has been made, executed or affixed with digital signature either by himself or by any other person, whether such person be living or dead at the time of such alteration; or

Thirdly - Who dishonestly or fraudulently causes any person to sign, seal, execute or alter a document or an electronic record or to affix his digital signature on any electronic record knowing that such person by reason of unsoundness of mind or intoxication cannot, or that by reason of deception practised upon him, he does not know the contents of the document or electronic record or the nature of the alterations.

IPC Section 468: Forgery for purpose of cheating

Whoever commits forgery, intending that the [document or Electronic Record forged] shall be used for the purpose of cheating, shall be punished with imprisonment of either description for a term which may extend to seven years, and shall also be liable to fine.

IPC Section 469: Forgery for purpose of harming reputation

Whoever commits forgery, [intending that the document or Electronic Record forged] shall harm the reputation of any party, or knowing that it is likely to used for that purpose, shall be punished with imprisonment of either description for a term which may extend to three years, and shall also be liable to fine.

IT Act 2008: Section 65: Tampering with Computer Source Documents

Whoever knowingly or intentionally conceals, destroys or alters or intentionally or knowingly causes another to conceal, destroy or alter any computer source code used for a computer, computer programme, computer system or computer network, when the computer source code is required to be kept or maintained by law for the time being in force, shall be punishable with imprisonment up to three years, or with fine which may extend up to two lakh rupees, or with both.

Explanation - For the purposes of this section, "Computer Source Code" means the listing of programmes, computer commands, design and layout and programme analysis of computer resource in any form.

Illustration 1

Mahesh Mhatre and Anand Khare (alias Dr Neukar) were arrested in 2002 for allegedly defacing the website of the Mumbai Cyber Crime Cell.

They had allegedly used password cracking software to crack the FTP password for the police website. They then replaced the homepage of the website with pornographic content. The duo was also charged with credit card fraud for using 225 credit card numbers, mostly belonging to American citizens.

Illustration 2

In 2001, over 200 Indian websites were hacked into and defaced. The hackers put in words like bugz, death symbol, Paki-king and allahhuakbar.

In the case of 123medicinindia.com, a message was left behind which said – "Catch me if uu can my deraz lazy adminzzz" –

challenging the system administrators to trace the miscreants. The offenders were allegedly a group of hackers who go by the name of 'Pakistani Cyber Warriors'.

Illustration 3

In 2006, a Turkish hacker using the handle iSKORPiTX was able to breach the security of a group of web servers, containing more than 38,500 web sites in less than a day!

Illustration 4

The first Defacers Challenge took place on Sunday, July 6, 2003. There was a special prize for the first contestant to deface 6,000 websites.

The contest was conducted over a six-hour period. Points were awarded based on the server's operating system.

Windows: 1 point,

Linux: 2 points,

BSD: 2 points.

AIX: 3 points

HP-UX: 5 points,

Macintosh: 5 points

E-mail Bombing

Email bombing refers to sending a large number of emails to the victim resulting in the victim's email account (in case of an individual) or mail servers (in case of a company or an email service provider) crashing.

Email bombing is a type of denial-of-service attack. A denial-of-service attack is one in which a flood of information requests is sent to a server, bringing the system to its knees and making the server difficult to access.

Section 66A: Punishment for sending offensive messages through communication service

Any person who sends, by means of a computer resource or a communication device,-

a) Any information that is grossly offensive or has menacing character; or b) any information which he knows to be false, but for the purpose of causing annoyance, inconvenience, danger, obstruction, insult, injury, criminal intimidation, enmity, hatred, or ill will, persistently makes by making use of such computer resource or a communication device, c) any electronic mail or electronic mail message for the purpose of causing annoyance or inconvenience or to deceive or to mislead the addressee or recipient about the origin of such messages shall be punishable with imprisonment for a term which may extend to three years and with fine.

Explanation: For the purposes of this section, terms "Electronic Mail" and "Electronic Mail Message" means a message or information created or transmitted or received on a computer, computer system, computer resource or communication device including attachments in text, image, audio, video and any other electronic record, which may be transmitted with the message.

Illustration 1

A British teenager was cleared of launching a denial-of-service attack against his former employer, in a ruling under the UK Computer Misuse Act.

The teenager was accused of sending 5 million e-mail messages to his ex-employer that caused the company's email server to crash. The judge held that the UK Computer Misuse Act does not specifically include a denial-of-service attack as a criminal offence.

Illustration 2

In one case, a foreigner who had been residing in Shimla, India for almost 30 years wanted to avail of a scheme introduced by the Shimla Housing Board to buy land at lower rates. When he made an application it was rejected on the grounds that the scheme was available only for citizens of India.

He decided to take his revenge. Consequently, he sent thousands of mails to the Shimla Housing Board and repeatedly kept sending e-mails till their servers crashed.

Data Diddling

One of the most common forms of computer crime is data diddling - illegal or unauthorized data alteration. These changes can occur before and during data input or before output. Data diddling cases have affected banks, payrolls, inventory records, credit records, school transcripts and virtually all other forms of data processing known.

Section 66 and 43(d) of the I.T. Act covers the offence of data diddling.

Section 66: Computer Related Offences

If any person, dishonestly, or fraudulently, does any act referred to in section 43, he shall be punishable with imprisonment for a term which may extend to two three years or with fine which may extend to five lakh rupees or with both.

Explanation: For the purpose of this section-

a) the word "dishonestly" shall have the meaning assigned to it in section 24 of the Indian Penal Code;

b) the word "fraudulently" shall have the meaning assigned to it in section 25 of the Indian Penal Code.

Section 43(d): damages or causes to be damaged any computer, computer system or computer network, data, computer database or any other programs residing in such computer, computer system or computer network;Case in point:

NDMC Electricity Billing Fraud Case: A private contractor who was to deal with receipt and accounting of electricity bills by the NDMC, Delhi. Collection of money, computerized accounting, record maintenance and remittance in his bank who misappropriated huge amount of funds by manipulating data files to show less receipt and bank remittance

Illustration 1

The NDMC Electricity Billing Fraud Case that took place in 1996 is a typical example. The computer network was used for receipt and accounting of electricity bills by the New Delhi Municipal Council. Collection of money, computerized accounting, record maintenance and remittance in the bank were exclusively left to a private contractor who was a computer professional.

He misappropriated huge amount of funds by manipulating data files to show less receipt and bank remittance.

Illustration 2

A keyboard operator processing orders at an Oakland USA department store changed some delivery addresses and diverted several thousand dollars-worth of store goods into the hands of accomplices.

Illustration 3

A ticket clerk at the Arizona Veterans' Memorial Coliseum in

USA issued full-price basketball tickets, sold them and then, tapping out codes on her computer keyboard, recorded the transactions as half-price sales.

Salami Attacks

These attacks are used for committing financial crimes. The key here is to make the alteration so insignificant that in a single case it would go completely unnoticed.

For instance, a bank employee inserts a program, into the bank's servers, that deducts a small amount of money (say Rs. 2 a month) from the account of every customer. No account holder will probably notice this unauthorized debit, but the bank employee will make a sizeable amount of money every month.

The attack is called "salami attack" as it is analogous to slicing the data thinly, like salami.

Illustration 1

Four executives of a rental-car franchise in Florida USA defrauded at least 47,000 customers using a salami technique. They modified a computer billing program to add five extra gallons to the actual gas tank capacity of their vehicles. From 1988 through 1991, every customer who returned a car without topping it off ended up paying inflated rates for an inflated total of gasoline.

The thefts ranged from $2 to $15 per customer -difficult for the victims to detect.

Illustration 2

In January 1997, Willis Robinson of Maryland USA, was

sentenced to 10 years in prison for "having reprogrammed his Taco Bell drive-up-window cash register - causing it to ring up each $2.99 item internally as a 1-cent item, so that he could pocket $2.98 each time".

The management assumed the error was hardware or software and only caught the perpetrator when he bragged about his crime to co-workers.

Illustration 3

In Los Angeles USA four men were charged with fraud for allegedly installing computer chips in gasoline pumps that cheated consumers by overstating the amounts pumped. The problem came to light when an increasing number of consumers claimed that they had been sold more gasoline than the capacity of their gas tanks!

However, the fraud was difficult to prove initially because the perpetrators programmed the chips to deliver exactly the right amount of gasoline when asked for five- and 10-gallon amounts (precisely the amounts typically used by inspectors).

Denial of Service Attack

Denial of Service attacks (DOS attacks) involves flooding a computer with more requests than it can handle. This causes the computer (e.g. a web server) to crash and results in authorized users being unable to access the service offered by the computer.

Another variation to a typical denial of service attack is known as a Distributed Denial of Service (DDoS) attack wherein the perpetrators are many and are geographically widespread.

Denial-of-service attacks have had an impressive history having, in the past, blocked out websites like Amazon, CNN, Yahoo and eBay. The attack is initiated by sending excessive demands to the victim's computer(s), exceeding the limit that the victim's servers can support and making the servers crash. Sometimes, many computers are entrenched in this process by installing a Trojan on them; taking control of them and then making them send numerous demands to the targeted computer.

Section 43 of ITA 2008 case will be filled.

Section 43: Penalty and Compensation for damage to computer, computer system

If any person without permission of the owner or any other person who is in-charge of a computer, computer system or computer network -

(a) accesses or secures access to such computer, computer system or computer network or computer resource

(b) downloads, copies or extracts any data, computer data base or information from such computer, computer system or computer network including information or data held or stored in any removable storage medium;

(c) introduces or causes to be introduced any computer contaminant or computer virus into any computer, computer system or computer network;

(d) damages or causes to be damaged any computer, computer system or computer network, data, computer data base or any other programmes residing in such computer, computer system or computer network;

(e) disrupts or causes disruption of any computer, computer system or computer network;

(f) denies or causes the denial of access to any person authorised to access any computer, computer system or computer network by any means;

(g) provides any assistance to any person to facilitate access to a computer, computer system or computer network in contravention of the provisions of this Act, rules or regulations made thereunder,

(h) charges the services availed of by a person to the account of another person by tampering with or manipulating any computer, computer system, or computer network,

(i) destroys, deletes or alters any information residing in a computer resource or diminishes its value or utility or affects it injuriously by any means

(ii) Steals, conceals, destroys or alters or causes any person to steal, conceal, destroy or alter any computer source code used for a computer resource with an intention to cause damage, he shall be liable to pay damages by way of compensation not exceeding one crore rupees to the person so affected. (Change vide ITAA 2008)

Explanation - for the purposes of this section -

(i) "Computer Contaminant" means any set of computer instructions that are designed -

(a) to modify, destroy, record, transmit data or programme residing within a computer, computer system or computer network; or

(b) by any means to usurp the normal operation of the computer, computer system, or computer network;

(ii) "Computer Database" means a representation of information, knowledge, facts, concepts or instructions in text, image, audio, video that are being prepared or have been prepared in a formalised manner or have been produced by a computer, computer system or computer network and are intended for use in a computer, computer system or computer network;

(iii) "Computer Virus" means any computer instruction, information, data or programme that destroys, damages, degrades or adversely affects the performance of a computer resource or attaches itself to another computer resource and operates when a programme, data or instruction is executed or some other event takes place in that computer resource;

(iv) "Damage" means to destroy, alter, delete, add, modify or re-arrange any computer resource by any means.

(v) "Computer Source code" means the listing of programmes, computer commands, design and layout and programme analysis of computer resource in any form (Inserted vide ITAA 2008)

Illustration 1

A series of distributed denial of service attacks in February 2000 crippled many popular websites including yahoo.com, amazon.com and cnn.com

Illustration 2

A series of more than 125 separate but coordinated denial-of -service attack hit the cyber infrastructure of Estonia in early 2007. The attacks were apparently connected with protests against the Estonian government's decision to remove a Soviet-era war memorial from the capital city. It is suspected that the attacks were carried out by Russian hackers. The attack lasted several days.

Spreading Virus / Worm Attack

Computer viruses are small software programs that are designed to spread from one computer to another and to interfere with computer operation. A virus might corrupt or delete data on the victim's computer, use the victim's e-mail program to spread itself to other computers, or even erase everything on the victim's hard disk.

Viruses are most easily spread by attachments in e-mail messages or instant messaging messages. Viruses can be disguised as attachments of funny images, greeting cards, or audio and video files.

Viruses can also spread through downloads on the Internet. They can be hidden in illicit software or other files or programs. Worms, unlike viruses do not need the host to attach themselves to. They merely make functional copies of themselves and do this repeatedly till they eat up all the available space on a computer's memory.

The term worm is sometimes used to mean self-replicating malware. These terms are often used interchangeably in the context of the hybrid viruses / worms that dominate the current virus scenario.

How does this happen?

The malicious code or virus is inserted into the chain of command so that when the infected program is run, the viral code is also executed (or in some cases, run instead of the legitimate program). Viruses are usually seen as extraneous code attached to a host program, but this isn't always the case. Sometimes, the environment is manipulated so that calling a legitimate uninfected program calls the viral program.

The viral program may also be executed before any other program is run. This can virtually infect every executable file on the computer, even though none of those files' code was actually tampered with. Viruses that follow this modus operandi include "cluster" or "FAT" viruses, which redirect system pointers to infected files, associate viruses and viruses that modify the Windows Registry directory entries so that their own code is executed before any other legitimate program.

Computer viruses usually spread via removable media or the Internet. A flash disk, CD-ROM, magnetic tape or other storage device that has been in an infected computer infects all future computers in which it is used. Your computer can also contract viruses from sinister email attachments, rogue web sites or infected software. And these disseminate to every other computer on your network.

All computer viruses cause direct or indirect economic damages. Based on this, there are two categories of viruses:

- Those that only disseminate and don't cause intentional damage.
- Those which are programmed to cause damage.

However, even by disseminating, they take up plenty of memory space, and time and resources that are spent on the clean-up job. Direct economic damages are caused when viruses alter the information during digital transmission. Considerable expenses are incurred by individuals, firms and authorities for developing and implementing the anti-virus tools to protect computer systems.

Brain (in its first incarnation written in January 1986) is considered to be the first computer virus for the PC. The virus is also known as Lahore, Pakistani, Pakistani Brain, Brain-A and UIUC. The virus was written by two brothers, Basit and Amjad Farooq Alvi, who lived in Lahore, Pakistan. The brothers told TIME magazine they had written it to protect their medical software from piracy and was supposed to target copyright infringers only.

The virus came complete with the brothers' address and three phone numbers, and a message that told the user that their machine was infected and for inoculation the user should call them.

When the brothers began to receive a large number of phone calls from people in USA, Britain, and elsewhere, demanding them to disinfect their machines, the brothers were stunned and tried to explain to the outraged callers that their motivation had not been malicious.

They ended up having to get their phone lines cut off and regretted that they had revealed their contact details in the first place. The brothers are still in business in Pakistan as internet service providers in their company called Brain Limited.

Introduces or causes to be introduced any viruses or contaminant in that case, suit filed under Chapter IX of IT Act i.e. Section 43 as a Civil Wrongs under IT Act

Section 66 and 43(c),(e) of the I.T. Act covers the offence of spreading virus and worm attack.

Section 66: Computer Related Offences

If any person, dishonestly, or fraudulently, does any act referred to in section 43, he shall be punishable with imprisonment for a term which may extend to two three years or with fine which may extend to five lakh rupees or with both.

Explanation: For the purpose of this section-

a) the word "dishonestly" shall have the meaning assigned to it in section 24 of the Indian Penal Code;

b) the word "fraudulently" shall have the meaning assigned to it in section 25 of the Indian Penal Code.

Section 43(c): If any person without permission of the owner or any other person who is in-charge of a computer, computer system or computer network - introduces or causes to be introduced any computer contaminant or computer virus into any computer, computer system or computer network;

Section 43(e): If any person without permission of the owner or any other person who is in-charge of a computer, computer system or computer network - disrupts or causes disruption of any computer, computer system or computer network;

he shall be liable to pay damages by way of compensation not exceeding one crore rupees to the person so affected. (Change vide ITAA 2008)

Illustration 1

The VBS_LOVELETTER virus (better known as the Love Bug or the ILOVEYOU virus) was reportedly written by a Filipino undergraduate. In May 2000, this deadly virus became the world's most prevalent virus. Losses incurred during this virus attack were pegged at US $ 10 billion.

VBS_LOVELETTER utilized the addresses in Microsoft Outlook and e-mailed itself to those addresses. The e-mail, which was sent out, had "ILOVEYOU" in its subject line. The attachment file was named "LOVE-LETTER-FORYOU.TXT.vbs".

People wary of opening e-mail attachments were conquered by the subject line and those who had some knowledge of viruses, did not notice the tiny .vbs extension and believed the file to be a text file. The message in the e-mail was "kindly check the attached LOVELETTER coming from me".

Illustration 2

Probably the world's most famous worm was the Internet worm let loose on the Internet by Robert Morris sometime in 1988. The Internet was, then, still in its developing years and this worm, which affected thousands of computers, almost brought its development to a complete halt. It took a team of experts almost three days to get rid of the worm and in the meantime many of the computers had to be disconnected from the network.

Illustration 3

In 2002, the creator of the Melissa computer virus was

convicted. The virus had spread in 1999 and caused more than $80 million in damage by disrupting personal computers, business and government computer networks.

Illustration 4

In 2006, a US citizen was convicted for conspiracy to intentionally cause damage to protected computers and commit computer fraud. Between 2004 and 2005, he created and operated the malicious software to constantly scan for and infect new computers.

It damaged hundreds of US Department of Defence computers in USA, Germany and Italy. The software compromised computer systems at a Seattle hospital, including patient systems, and damaged more than 1,000 computers in a California school district.

Illustration 5

Logic bombs are event dependent programs. This implies that these programs are created to do something only when a certain event (known as a trigger event) occurs. E.g. even some viruses may be termed logic bombs because they lie dormant all through the year and become active only on a particular date (like the Chernobyl virus).

Trojans and Keyloggers

A Trojan, as this program is aptly called, is an unauthorized program which functions from inside what seems to be an authorized program, thereby concealing what it is actually doing.

Trojan Horses are different from viruses in their manner of propagation. They masquerade as a legitimate file, such as an email attachment from a supposed friend with a very believable name, and don't disseminate themselves. The user can also unknowingly install a Trojan-infected program via drive-by downloads when visiting a website, playing online games or using internet-driven applications. A Trojan Horse can also cause damage similar to other viruses such as steal information or hamper / disrupt the functioning of computer systems.

Types of Trojans

The following are the most common types of Trojan:

1. Remote Administration Trojans (RATs) - Modern RATs are very simple to use. They come packaged with two files - the server file and the client file. The hacker tricks someone into running the server file, gets his IP address and gets full control over his/her computer. Some Trojans are limited by their functions, but more functions also mean larger server files. Some Trojans are merely meant for the attacker to use them to upload another Trojan to his target's computer and run it; hence they take very little disk space.

Hackers also bind Trojans into other programs, which appear to be legitimate e.g. a RAT could be bound with an e-greeting card. There are many programs that detect common Trojans.

Firewalls and anti-virus software can be useful in tracing RATs.

2. Password Trojans – Password Trojans search the victim's computer for passwords and then send them to the attacker or the author of the Trojan.

Whether it's an Internet password or an e-mail password there is a Trojan for every password. These Trojans usually send the information back to the attacker via E-mail.

3. Privileges-Elevating Trojans - These Trojans are usually used to fool system administrators. They can either be bound into a common system utility or pretend to be something harmless and even quite useful and appealing. Once the administrator runs it, the Trojan will give the attacker more privileges on the system. These Trojans can also be sent to less-privileges users and give the attacker access to their account.

4. Destructive Trojans - These Trojans can destroy the victim's entire hard drive, encrypt or just scramble important files. Some might seem like joke programs, while they are actually ripping every file they encounter to pieces.

Some common Trojans

5. Back Orifice (BO) - This Trojan was developed by a community of hackers known as "Cult of the dead cow" (www.cultdeadcow.com). This Trojan can be downloaded from www.BO2K.com and numerous other websites. (Note: the websites keep changing and it is best to use a powerful search engine like www.Google.com to search for the program.)

Back Orifice consists of two parts, a client application and a server application (approximately 122 KB). The client application, running on the hacker's computer, can be used to monitor and control the victim's computer (which runs the server application). The hacker can do the following activities on the victim's computer:

- Run any program or see any file
- Keep a record of all the keys punched on the keyboard
- Shutdown or restart the victim's computer
- Transfer files to or from the victim computer

The hacker could be in Australia and the victim in China, but still the hacker can do all the above activities on the victim's computer! The following are the main characteristics of BO:

- BO can only be used on victim computers that are running the Windows 95 or Windows 98 operating systems.
- The server part of the program has to be installed on the victim computer. The victim is usually fooled into installing the server part by sending him the Trojan fused with another program (e.g. an electronic Diwali card fused with the Trojan program).
- The hacker needs to know the IP address of the victim computer.
- If the victim computer is behind a firewall, then BO will not work

6. NetBus - NetBus was developed by a Swedish citizen named Carl-Fredrik Neikter who claimed that he developed it "purely for fun". Netbus can be downloaded from hundreds of websites. It is best to use Google.com to search for the program. Netbus allows the hacker to do numerous activities on the victim's computer. Some of these are:

- Open/close the CD-ROM once or in intervals (specified in seconds)
- Swap mouse buttons - the right mouse button works like the left mouse button and vice versa.
- Start any program.
- Play any sound-file (it supports only WAV files).
- Point the mouse to some other place. The hacker can navigate the victim's mouse with his own.
- Show a message dialogue on the screen. The answer is sent back to the hacker. The hacker can ask for the password and the victim would enter it!
- Shutdown or log off the victim.
- Open any website.
- Type anything in the program that the victim is using.
- Obtain a list of all the keys on the keyboard that the victim is punching.
- Get an image of the screen (called a screen dump).
- Get information about the victim computer.
- Upload any file to the victim computer. Using this feature the hacker can upload any virus or Trojan or update the Netbus Trojan itself.
- Increase and decrease the sound-volume.
- Record sounds that the microphone can catch. The sound is sent to the hacker.
- Make click sounds every time a key is pressed.
- Download and delete any file on the victim computer.
- Disable keys on the victim keyboard.

The following are the main characteristics of Netbus:

- Once it is installed on the victim computer, it runs every time the computer is started.
- Netbus can be used on victim computers that are running the Windows 95 or Windows 98 or Windows NT operating systems.

Keyloggers are regularly used were to log all the strokes a victim makes on the keyboard. This assumes sinister proportions, if a key logger is installed on a computer which is regularly used for online banking and other financial transactions. Keyloggers are most commonly found in public computers such as those in cyber cafes, hotels etc. Unsuspecting victims also end up downloading spyware when they click on "friendly" offers for free software.

Illustration 1

A young lady reporter was working on an article about online relationships. The article focused on how people can easily find friendship and even love on the Internet. During the course of her research she made a lot of online friends. One of these 'friends' managed to infect her computer with a Trojan.

This young lady stayed in a small one bedroom apartment and her computer was located in one corner of her bedroom. Unknown to her, the Trojan would activate her web camera and microphone even when the Internet was switched off. A year later she realized that hundreds of her pictures were posted on pornographic sites around the world!

Illustration 2

The network administrator in a global bank received a

beautifully packed CD ROM containing "security updates" from the company that developed the operating system that ran his bank's servers.

He installed the "updates" which in reality was Trojanized software. 3 years later, the effects were still being felt in the bank's system!

Internet Time Theft

This connotes the usage by an unauthorized person of the Internet hours paid for by another person.

Illustration

In May 2000, the Delhi police arrested an engineer who had misused the login name and password of a customer whose Internet connection he had set up.

The case was filed under the Indian Penal Code and the Indian Telegraph Act.

Theft of Computer Hardware

Section 43 of IT Act 2008 and also under Sec. 378, 379 IPC

Section 43: Penalty and Compensation for damage to computer, computer system

If any person without permission of the owner or any other person who is in-charge of a computer, computer system or computer network -

(a) accesses or secures access to such computer, computer system or computer network or computer resource

(b) downloads, copies or extracts any data, computer data base or information from such computer, computer system or computer network including information or data held or stored in any removable storage medium;

(c) introduces or causes to be introduced any computer contaminant or computer virus into any computer, computer system or computer network;

(d) damages or causes to be damaged any computer, computer system or computer network, data, computer data base or any other programmes residing in such computer, computer system or computer network;

(e) disrupts or causes disruption of any computer, computer system or computer network;

(f) denies or causes the denial of access to any person authorised to access any computer, computer system or computer network by any means;

(g) provides any assistance to any person to facilitate access to a computer, computer system or computer network in contravention of the provisions of this Act, rules or regulations made there under,

(h) charges the services availed of by a person to the account of another person by tampering with or manipulating any computer, computer system, or computer network,

(i) destroys, deletes or alters any information residing in a computer resource or diminishes its value or utility or affects it injuriously by any means

(i) Steals, conceals, destroys or alters or causes any person to steal, conceal, destroy or alter any computer source code used for a computer resource with an intention to cause damage, he shall be liable to pay damages by way of compensation not exceeding one crore rupees to the person so affected.(change vide ITAA 2008)

Explanation - for the purposes of this section -

(i) "Computer Contaminant" means any set of computer instructions that are designed -

(a) to modify, destroy, record, transmit data or program residing within a computer, computer system or computer network; or

(b) by any means to usurp the normal operation of the computer, computer system, or computer network;

(ii) "Computer Database" means a representation of information, knowledge, facts, concepts or instructions in text, image, audio, video that are being prepared or have been prepared in a formalised manner or have been produced by a computer, computer system or computer network and are intended for use in a computer, computer system or computer network;

(iii) "Computer Virus" means any computer instruction, information, data or program that destroys, damages, degrades or adversely affects the performance of a computer resource or attaches itself to another computer resource and operates when a program, data or instruction is executed or some other event takes place in that computer resource;

(iv) "Damage" means to destroy, alter, delete, add, modify or re-arrange any computer resource by any means.

(v) "Computer Source code" means the listing of programs, computer commands, design and layout and program analysis of computer resource in any form (Inserted vide ITAA 2008)

IPC Section 378: Theft

Whoever intending to take dishonestly any moveable property

out of the possession of any person without that person's consent, moves that property in order to such taking, is said to commit theft.

Explanation 1

A thing so long as it is attached to the earth, not being movable property, is not the subject of theft; but it becomes capable of being the subject of theft as soon as it is severed from the earth.

Explanation 2

A moving effected by the same act which affects the severance may be a theft.

Explanation 3

A person is said to cause a thing to move by removing an obstacle which prevented it from moving or by separating it from any other thing, as well as by actually moving it.

Explanation 4

A person, who by any means causes an animal to move, is said to move that animal, and to move everything which, in consequence of the motion so caused, is moved by that animal.

Explanation 5

The consent mentioned in the definition may be express or implied, and may be given either by the person in possession, or by any person having for the purpose authority either express or implied.

IPC Section 379: Punishment for theft

Whoever commits theft shall be punished with imprisonment of either description for a term which may extend to three years, or with fine, or with both.

Web Jacking

Just as conventional hijacking of an airplane is done by using force, similarly web jacking means forcefully taking over control of a website. The motive is usually the same as hijacking – ransom. The perpetrators have either a monetary or political purpose which they try to satiate by holding the owners of the website to ransom.

This occurs when someone forcefully takes control of a website (by cracking the password and later changing it). The actual owner of the website does not have any more control over what appears on that website.

How does web jacking take place?

The administrator of any website has a password and a username that only he (or someone authorized by him) may use to upload files from his computer on the web server (simply put, a server is a powerful computer) where his website is hosted.

Ideally, this password remains secret with the administrator. If a hacker gets hold of this username and password, then he can pretend to be the administrator.

Computers don't recognize people – only usernames and passwords. The web server will grant control of the website to whoever enters the correct password and username combination.

There are many ways in which a hacker may get to know a

password, the most common being password cracking wherein a "cracking software" is used to guess a password. Password cracking attacks are most commonly of two types:

The first one is known as the dictionary attack. In this type of attack the software will attempt all the words contained in a predefined dictionary of words. For example, it may try Rahim, Rahul, Rakesh, Ram, Reema, Reena ... in a predefined dictionary of Indian names. These types of dictionaries are readily available on the Internet.

The other form of password cracking is by using 'brute force'. In this kind of attack the software tries to guess the password by trying out all possible combinations of numbers, symbols, and letters till the correct password is found. For example, it may try out password combinations like abc123, acbd5679, sdj#%^, weuf*(-)*.

Some software, available for password cracking using the brute force technique, can check a huge number of password combinations per second.

When compared with a dictionary attack, a brute force attack takes more time, but it is definitely more successful.

Section 65 of ITA 2008

Section 65: Tampering with Computer Source Documents

Whoever knowingly or intentionally conceals, destroys or alters or intentionally or knowingly causes another to conceal, destroy or alter any computer source code used for a computer, computer programme, computer system or computer network, when the computer source code is required to be kept or maintained by law for the time being in force, shall be punishable with imprisonment up to three years, or with fine which may extend up to two lakh rupees, or with both.

Explanation -

For the purposes of this section, "Computer Source Code" means the listing of programs, Computer Commands, Design and layout and program analysis of computer resource in any form.

IPC Section 383: Extortion

Whoever intentionally puts any person in fear of any injury to that person, or to any other, and thereby dishonestly induces the person so put in fear to deliver to any property or valuable security, or anything signed or sealed which may be converted into a valuable security, commits "extortion".

IPC Section 384: Punishment for extortion

Whoever commits extortion shall be punished with imprisonment of either description for a term which may extend to three years, or with fine or with both.

Classification of Offence:

Punishment - Imprisonment for 3 years, or fine, or both – Cognizable - Non-bailable - Triable by any Magistrate - Non-compoundable

Illustration

In an incident reported in the USA, the owner of a hobby website for children received an e-mail informing her that a group of hackers had gained control over her website. They demanded a ransom of 1 million dollars from her. The owner, a schoolteacher, did not take the threat seriously. She felt that it was just a scare tactic and ignored the e-mail. It was three days later that she came to know, following many telephone calls from all over the country, that the hackers had web jacked her website. Subsequently, they had altered a portion of the website which was entitled 'How to have fun with goldfish'.

In all the places where it had been mentioned, they had replaced the word 'goldfish' with the word 'piranhas'.

Piranhas are tiny but extremely dangerous flesh-eating fish. Many children had visited the popular website and had believed what the contents of the website suggested.

These unfortunate children followed the instructions, tried to play with piranhas, which they bought from pet shops, and were very seriously injured.

E-mail Frauds

Dear Mr. Justin Williams, I'm Vikas Manjit Singh from Punjab (India). I belong to a city named Ludhiana. Mr. Williams, I am having a brother in Canada who is also named Justin Williams. He was adopted from my parents by some Mr. William Ram of Welland. Me and my mummy came over to Canada to leave Justin to his new family (William Ram's Family). It happened in June 1985.

So Mr. Justin Williams, if you are the same person I'm talking about. Then please give me some time so that I can let you know the realities.

Imagine the thoughts going through Mr. Justin William's head after reading this email. Is he really adopted? Where are his birth parents? Is this email from his birth brother?

In reality, this is a scam email originating from a college in Sangroor (India)!

Canadian citizens are targeted with these emails. If the targets start believing the sender to be their brother, they are asked to send money so that their "brother" can travel to Canada with the proof of the victim's adoption!

This is just one of the hundreds of email scams being perpetrated on the Internet.

These scams are commonly referred to as Nigerian 419 scams.

These scam emails are believed to originate from Nigeria and section 419 of the Nigerian Penal Code relates to cheating (like the famous section 420 of the Indian Penal Code).

In 2007 conducted a 3 month intensive investigation of hundreds of scam emails.

The results were very surprising to say the least. Less than 10% of these emails had actually originated from Nigeria!

A majority of these emails (more than 60%) have originated from Israel, followed by the Netherlands, UK and other European countries. The "birth brother" email was the only one originating from India.

Most of these scam emails promise the receiver millions (or sometimes billions) of dollars. Most commonly the email says that some rich African bureaucrat or businessman or politician has died and left behind a lot of money.

The scamster states that the Government is going to confiscate the money. The only way out is to transfer the money to the bank account of the email recipient.

All that the email recipient has to do is send his bank account details. For this a generous fee of a few million dollars will be paid!

If someone actually falls for this scam and provides the bank details, he is sent some official looking documents relating to the bank transfer of a huge sum of money. Once the victim is convinced of the "genuineness" of the transaction, something appears to go wrong.

The victim is informed that a small amount of money (ranging from US$ 100 to 2500) is needed for bank charges or other paper work. This money is the motive behind the elaborate scam. Once the victim pays this money, the scamster disappears from the scene.

The lottery scam emails inform the recipient that he has won a million dollar lottery run by Microsoft, Yahoo or some other well-known global company. The winner is asked to provide his bank details and pay a small sum for bank charges and other processing fees.

Another scam email begins with "This is to inform you that we are in possession of a consignment, deposited by British National Lottery which is to be couriered to you". The email asks for 470 pounds to be sent to the courier company so that the cheque for the lottery prize can be sent.

Another scam email comes with the subject line "Blessed is the hand that giveth". The sender claims to be a widow on her deathbed. She wants to donate her wealth to someone who will pray for her.

Another scam email comes from an "employee of the Euro Lottery". The "employee" claims to be in a position to carry out a lottery fraud and is willing to share the money with the email recipient.

What is common in all these scams is that scanned versions of official documents are emailed to potential victims. Once the victim is convinced of the genuineness of the transaction, a small fee is requested for meeting bank charges / legal fees / courier charges etc. It is this small fee that is the motive behind the scam.

It is believed that thousands of people are defrauded of billions of dollars every year through these scams.

Hacking of the E-mail Account:

The e-mail account of the victim is hacked by using various tools to capture the password of the account. This can be achieved by:

- Sending phishing emails purportedly from genuine email accounts of the email service (but actually fake). The email contains links that prompt you to visit a page for updating your password and other credentials on the pretext of some system update, data loss, technology upgrade, regulatory compliance, etc. The links direct you to a fake page where, once you enter your login ID and password the same get stealthily stolen by the fraudsters.
- Sending you unsolicited / spam mails containing attachments that have malwares embedded in them. Once such emails are opened and attachments activated the malware gets discreetly downloaded and installed on your device. The malware could be a keylogger that captures and sends all the keyboard taps to the fraudsters, which includes your account passwords. The other possible malwares could be ones that capture screenshot or read and transmit saved passwords.
- Email accounts having 2-factor authentication can also be got hacked when users share their OTP with fraudsters after getting tricked by social engineering tools.

Once an email account has been hacked the criminal case can misuse the account for the following purposes:

- Sending SOS mails to all your contacts asking for money citing some emergency such as passport, wallet etc. getting stolen in a foreign country, etc.

- Sending offensive messages to your friends and relatives or asking for some ransom for not sending such offensive messages.
- Sending mails to your clients and customers asking for payment of dues / remittances in a different bank account, thus swindling with your money.
- Using the unauthorized access to your email to gain access to your other online accounts, such as other email accounts, net-banking accounts, social media accounts, etc.

Preventive Measures / Precautions:

- Use two-factor authentication. Two-factor identification requires you to enter a code sent to you in a text message or another service to access your account after you enter your user name and password. This makes it more difficult for a hacker to access your information, even if they are able to crack your password.
- Do not open SPAM mails or e-mails sent from unknown senders. Do not click on any link sent on such mails.
- Be cautions while opening links sent in unsolicited e-mails even if they are sent from someone in your contact-list. Such known contacts' email account may have been compromised and thereafter used to send malicious codes to unsuspecting contacts.
- Do not click on attractive and tempting links sent over a WhatsApp message or routine SMS. They may lead you to malicious pages and cause malware intrusion on your system/device. Hackers use social engineering to trick you in clicking the links. Don't fall for it.
- Keep your e-mail password long and difficult. Password should have at least 8 characters and there should be at

least one upper-case, one lower-case, one numeral and one special character in your password.

- Don't store your passwords in your device (phone/tablet. etc). Anyone getting access (physical or remote) to your device will easily get to know your passwords.
- Don't disclose your password to anyone and keep changing it at regular intervals (2-4 months).
- Always have a lock screen on your smartphone, tablet, laptop, etc. protected by a PIN or password. Do not keep your device open and unattended even for a minute, especially in public places and your workplace.

Section 420: Cheating and dishonestly inducing delivery of property

Whoever cheats and thereby dishonestly induces the person deceived any property to any person, or to make, alter or destroy the whole or any part of a valuable security, or anything which is signed or sealed, and which is capable of being converted into a valuable security, shall be punished with imprisonment of either description for a term which may extend to seven years, and shall also be liable to fine.

Criminal Breach of Trust / Fraud – IPC Section 405, 406, 408, 409

Illustration 1

In 2005, an Indian businessman received an email from the Vice President of a major African bank offering him a lucrative contract in return for a kickback of Rs 1 million.

The businessman had many telephonic conversations with the sender of the e-mail. He also verified the email address of the

'Vice President' from the website of the bank and subsequently transferred the money to the bank account mentioned in the email. It later turned out that the email was a spoofed one and was actually sent by an Indian based in Nigeria.

Illustration 2

A new type of scam e-mail threatens to kill recipients if they do not pay thousands of dollars to the sender, who purports to be a hired assassin. Replying to the e-mails just sends a signal to senders that they've reached a live account. It also escalates the intimidation.

In one case, a recipient threatened to call authorities. The scammer, who was demanding $20,000, reiterated the threat and sent some personal details about the recipient - address, daughter's full name etc. He gave an ultimatum: "TELL ME NOW ARE YOU READY TO DO WHAT I SAID OR DO YOU WANT ME TO PROCEED WITH MY JOB? ANSWER YES/NO AND DON'T ASK ANY QUESTIONS!!!"

Some emails claim to be from the FBI in London and inform recipients that an arrest was made in the case.

The e-mail says the recipient's information was found with the suspect and that they should reply to assist in the investigation. These emails are part of the scam!

Cyber Terrorism

Computer crime has hit mankind with unbelievable severity. Computer viruses, worms, Trojans, denial of service attacks, spoofing attacks and e-frauds have taken the real and virtual worlds by storm.

However, all these pale in the face of the most dreaded threat – that of cyber terrorism has defined cyber terrorism as:

"Cyber terrorism is the premeditated use of disruptive activities, or the threat thereof, in cyber space, with the intention to further social, ideological, religious, political or similar objectives, or to intimidate any person in furtherance of such objectives."

Over recent decades, it has become apparent that our society is becoming increasingly information technology dependent. Though many of us utilise technology for our own benefit, in aiding and supporting our lives in many ways, it also introduces many differing risks and vulnerabilities to our society. Those who use computer technology to commit crimes and acts of terror pose an alarming threat across the globe as we become ever more dependent on information technology. The use of computer technology and cyber-dependent attacks is becoming a more prominent threat by terrorist groups; this emerging threat defines itself as cyber terrorism.

Areas of Cyber Terrorism:

As discussed many acts of cyber terrorism are often synonymous with acts of cybercrime. Thus the means by which attacks are implemented by terrorists may also be done by criminals. These can come in many forms, as attacks are often either un-targeted or targeted. These can include, but not limited to:

Un-targeted Attacks

- **Phishing**: These attacks typically involve fraudulent emails to convince a target of its legitimacy of a user or organisation in order to attain private information (e.g., passwords, banking information, identity theft etc.)
- **Watering Hole**: The deployment of a fake webpage to compromise the original, in order to attack visiting users (e.g. the downloading of Remote Access Tools)
- **Ransomware**: Infecting a system by encrypting files and / or locking the user's access to said system. Then requiring a 'ransom' to gain normal access again.
- **Scanning**: Testing for vulnerabilities in specific internet networks or systems to deploy attacks on a wider scale to attack at random.

Targeted Attacks

- **Spear-Phishing**: These attacks are much the same as Phishing (mentioned in the Un-targeted attacks), however specifically targeted at an individual or organisation.
- **Distributed Denial of Service**: This is to deploy a mass amount of packet requests, often from a Botnet, to a website or network in order to overload the system and prevent regular access by legitimate users.

- **Supply Chain**: Attacking an element of an organisation before it arrives.
- **Zero Day**: Bespoke exploitation of a system with specific vulnerabilities not yet known to the author.

IT Act 2008: Section 66F: Cyber Terrorism

(1) Whoever,-

(A) with intent to threaten the unity, integrity, security or sovereignty of India or to strike terror in the people or any section of the people by –

(i) denying or cause the denial of access to any person authorized to access computer resource; or

(ii) attempting to penetrate or access a computer resource without authorization or exceeding authorized access; or

(iii) introducing or causing to introduce any Computer Contaminant and by means of such conduct causes or is likely to cause death or injuries to persons or damage to or destruction of property or disrupts or knowing that it is likely to cause damage or disruption of supplies or services essential to the life of the community or adversely affect the critical information infrastructure specified under section 70, or

(B) knowingly or intentionally penetrates or accesses a computer resource without authorisation or exceeding authorized access, and by means of such conduct obtains access to information, data or computer database that is restricted for reasons of the security of the State or foreign relations; or any restricted information, data or computer database, with reasons to believe that such information, data or computer database so obtained may be used to cause or likely to cause injury to the interests of the sovereignty and integrity of India, the security of the State, friendly relations with foreign States, public order, decency or morality, or in relation to contempt of court, defamation or incitement to an offence, or to the advantage of any foreign nation, group of individuals or otherwise, commits the offence of cyber terrorism.

(2) Whoever commits or conspires to commit cyber terrorism shall be punishable with imprisonment which may extend to imprisonment for life'.

Illustration 1

In 1996, a computer hacker allegedly associated with the White Supremacist movement temporarily disabled a US based Internet Service Provider (ISP) and damaged part of its record keeping system.

The ISP had attempted to stop the hacker from sending out worldwide racist messages under the ISP's name. The hacker signed off with the threat, "you have yet to see true electronic terrorism. This is a promise."

Illustration 2

In 1998, Spanish protestors bombarded the Institute for Global Communications (IGC) with thousands of bogus e-mail messages. E-mail was tied up and undeliverable to the ISP's users, and support lines were tied up with people who couldn't get their mail. The protestors also spammed IGC staff and member accounts, clogged their Web page with bogus credit card orders, and threatened to employ the same tactics against organizations using IGC services.

They demanded that IGC stop hosting the website for the Euskal Herria Journal, a New York-based publication supporting Basque independence. Protestors said IGC supported terrorism because a section on the Web pages contained materials on the terrorist group ETA, which claimed responsibility for assassinations of Spanish political and security officials, and attacks on military installations. IGC finally relented and pulled the site because of the "mail bombings."

Illustration 3

In 1998, a 12-year-old boy successfully hacked into the controls for the huge Roosevelt Dam on the Salt River in Arizona, USA.

He might have released floodwaters that would have inundated Mesa and Tempe, endangering at least 1 million people.

Illustration 4

In 2005, US security consultants reported that hackers were targeting the U.S. electric power grid and had gained access to U.S. utilities' electronic control systems.

Illustration 5

In 1998, ethnic Tamil guerrillas swamped Sri Lankan embassies with 800 e-mails a day over a two-week period. The messages read "We are the Internet Black Tigers and we're doing this to disrupt your communications." Intelligence authorities characterized it as the first known attack by terrorists against a country's computer systems.

Illustration 6

During the Kosovo conflict in 1999, NATO computers were blasted with e-mail bombs and hit with denial-of-service attacks by hacktivists protesting the NATO bombings.

In addition, businesses, public organizations, and academic institutes received highly politicized virus-laden e-mails from a range of Eastern European countries, according to reports. Web defacements were also common.

Illustration 7

Since December 1997, the Electronic Disturbance Theatre (EDT) has been conducting Web sit-ins against various sites in support of the Mexican Zapatistas.

At a designated time, thousands of protestors point their browsers to a target site using software that floods the target with rapid and repeated download requests.

EDT's software has also been used by animal rights groups against organizations said to abuse animals. Electrohippies, another group of hacktivists, conducted Web sit-ins against the WTO when they met in Seattle in late 1999.

Illustration 8

In 1994, a 16-year-old English boy took down some 100 U.S. defence systems.

Illustration 9

In 1997, 35 computer specialists used hacking tools freely available on 1,900 web sites to shut down large segments of the US power grid. They also silenced the command and control system of the Pacific Command in Honolulu.

Illustration 10

In 2001, in the backdrop of the downturn in US-China relationships, the Chinese hackers released the Code Red virus into the wild. This virus infected millions of computers around the world and then used these computers to launch denial of service attacks on US web sites, prominently the web site of the White House.

Illustration 11

In 2001, hackers broke into the U.S. Justice Department's web site and replaced the department's seal with a swastika, dubbed the agency the "United States Department of Injustice" and filled the page with obscene pictures.

Illustration 12:

The Mumbai police have registered a case of "cyber terrorism", the first in the state since an amendment to the Information Technology Act, where a threat email was sent to the BSE and NSE on Monday. The MRA Marg police and the Cyber Crime Investigation Cell are jointly probing the case. The suspect has been detained in this case. The police said an email challenging the security agencies to prevent a terror attack was sent by one Shahab Md with an ID sh.itaiyeb125@yahoo.in to BSE's administrative email ID corp.relations@bseindia.com at around 10.44 am on Monday. The IP address of the sender has been traced to Patna in Bihar. The ISP is Sify. The email ID was created just four minutes before the email was sent. "The sender had, while creating the new ID, given two mobile numbers in the personal details column. Both the numbers belong to a photo frame-maker in Patna." said an officer. **Status:** The MRA Marg police have registered forgery for purpose of cheating, criminal intimidation cases under the IPC and a cyber-terrorism case under the IT Act.

Encryption

A disturbing trend that is emerging nowadays is the increasing use of encryption, high frequency encrypted voice / data links, steganography40 etc. by terrorists and members of organized crime cartels. Notable examples are those of Osama bin Laden, Ramsey Yousef, Leary, the Cali carte, the Dutch underworld and the Italian mafia. Strong encryption is the criminal's best friend and the policeman's worst enemy. If a criminal were to use 512-bit symmetric encryption, how long would it take to decrypt the information using brute force techniques?

Current encryption regulations; India currently does not have any generally applicable restrictions on encryption. What it does have though is sectoral restrictions in areas such as telecom, as well as enabling laws that empower the government to issue general restrictions if it wants to. Entities holding telecom licences in India (whether they're pure internet service providers such as ACT Fibernet or full-fledged telcos such as Airtel or Vodafone) are subject to the most extensive encryption regulations. Most notably, they are prohibited from deploying 'bulk encryption' (a term that the Department of Telecom has unhelpfully left undefined) on their networks. Some telecom licences and associated guidance documents, including for telecom services such as international long distance (ILD) which carry all of India's inbound and outbound internet and voice traffic, also contain an anachronistic provision restricting encryption key lengths to 40-bits.

Sectoral regulators such as the Reserve Bank of India or the Securities and Exchange Board of India have, on the other hand, thankfully gone in the other direction. They mandate minimum encryption standards for entities and transactions, acknowledging the key role played by encryption in enabling trust and security.

Separate from this, the Information Technology Act, 2000 (IT Act) contains a framework for more general regulation. Section 84A empowers the government to "prescribe modes or methods for encryption" by issuing rules. This was attempted in 2015 when the Ministry of Electronics & IT (MeitY) issued a disastrous 'draft encryption policy', which was withdrawn almost immediately due to a strong private sector and civil society opposition (along with, perhaps, the realisation that it was completely unworkable). While there have been rumours of a MeitY committee tasked with producing a new draft, there is no clarity on it or when such a draft will be released.

The IT Act also contains another wide provision in Section 69, which allows the government to issue directions for 'decryption of any information generated, transmitted, received or stored in any computer resource'. Crucially, under this provision, an 'intermediary' (a wide term which covers Telco's, online communications and social networking services, and others) is obliged to assist the government in any manner directed. Failure to do so can lead to fines and imprisonment of up to seven years. Interestingly, this provision appears never to have been used by the government, at least based on publicly available information.

Illustration 1

Leary, who was sentenced to 94 years in prison for setting off fire bombs in the New York (USA) subway system in 1995, had developed his own algorithm for encrypting the files on his computer.

Illustration 2

The Cali cartel is reputed to be using:

- Sophisticated encryption to conceal their telephone communications
- Radios that distort voices, video phones which provide visual authentication of the caller's identity
- Instruments for scrambling transmission from computer modems

Illustration 3

The Italian mafia is believed to use PGP (Pretty Good Privacy) software for symmetric as well as asymmetric encryption.

Illustration 4

On March 20, 1995, the Aum Supreme Truth cult dropped bags of sarin nerve gas in the Tokyo subway, killing 12 people and injuring 6,000 more. Members of the cult had developed many chemical and biological weapons, including Sarin, VX, Mustard gas, Cyanide, botulism, anthrax and Q fever. It is believed that preparations were underway to develop nuclear capability. The cult was also believed to be developing a "death ray" that could destroy all life!

The records of the cult had been stored in encrypted form (using the RSA algorithm) on computers. The enforcement authorities were able to decrypt the information as the relevant private key was found in a floppy disk seized from the cult's premises. The encrypted information related to plans of the cult to cause mass deaths in Japan and USA.

Illustration 5

In 1997, a Bolivian terrorist organization had assassinated four U.S. army personnel. A raid on one of the hideouts of the terrorist's yielded information encrypted using symmetric encryption. A 12-hour brute force attack resulted in the decryption of the information and subsequently led to one of the largest drug busts in Bolivian history and the arrest of the terrorists.

Illustration 6

James Bell was arrested for violating internal revenue laws of the USA. He did this by:

- collecting the names and home addresses of agents and employees of the Internal Revenue Service (IRS) of the USA in order to intimidate them
- soliciting people to join in a scheme known as "Assassination Politics". Under this scheme those who killed selected government employees, including tax collectors, would be rewarded;
- using false Social Security Numbers to hide his assets and avoid taxes;
- contaminating an area outside IRS premises in many states of the USA with Mercaptan (a stink gas).

Investigators found on his computer documents relating to a

plan to destroy electronic equipment with nickel-plated carbon fiber.

They also found an invoice for the purchase of the fiber at his residence, and a bundle of the material at the residence of his associate, Robert East. Bell had exchanged PGP-encrypted e-mail messages with some of his associates.

As part of his plea bargain, he turned over the passphrase to his private key. This allowed investigators to decrypt messages that he had received.

Illustration 7

Dutch organized crime syndicates use PGP and PGPfone to encrypt their communications. They also use palmtop computers installed with Secure Device, a Dutch software product for encrypting data with International Data Encryption Algorithm (IDEA).

In 1995, the Amsterdam Police captured a PC in possession of one organized crime member. The PC contained an encrypted partition, which they were able to recover only in 1997.

Illustration 8

An encryption case occurring in Vilseck, West Germany involved theft, fraud, and embezzlement of U.S. defense contractor and U.S. government funds from 1986 to 1988.

The accused had stored financial records relating to the crimes on a personal computer, the hard disk of which had been password protected.

The police used hacking software to defeat the password protection, only to find that some of the files listed in the directory had been encrypted.

They then found the encryption program on the hard disk and used brute force tools to decrypt the files.

Illustration 9

The Dallas Police Department in the USA encountered encryption in the investigation of a drug ring, which was operating in several states of the USA and dealing in Ecstasy.

A member of the ring, residing within their jurisdiction, had encrypted his address book. He turned over the password, enabling the police to decrypt the file.

Meanwhile, however, the accused was out on bail and alerted his associates, so the decrypted information was not as useful as it might have been.

The police noted that Ecstasy dealers were more knowledgeable about computers when compared with other types of drug dealers, most likely because they were younger and better educated.

Illustration 10

Kevin Poulson was a skilled hacker who rigged radio contests and burglarized telephone-switching offices and hacked into the telephone network in order to determine whose phone was being tapped and to install his own phone tapping devices.

Poulson had encrypted files documenting everything from

the phone tapping he had discovered to the dossiers he had compiled about his enemies. The files had been encrypted several times using the Data Encryption Standard.

A US Department of Energy supercomputer took several months to find the key, at a cost of millions of dollars. The result yielded nearly ten thousand pages of evidence.

Illustration 11

The mother of a 15-year old boy filed a complaint against an adult who had sold her son US $1000 worth of hardware and software for one dollar.

The man had also given the boy lewd pictures on floppy disks.

The man subsequently mailed the boy pornographic material on floppy disks and sent pornographic files over the Internet.

When the accused was arrested it was found out that he had encrypted a directory on the system using PGP. The police were never able to decrypt the files.

Phishing

This is a technique of extracting confidential information such as credit card numbers and username password combos by masquerading as a legitimate enterprise. Phishing is typically carried out by email spoofing. You've probably received email containing links to legitimate appearing websites. You probably found it suspicious and didn't click on the link. Smart Move!!!

The malware would have installed itself on your computer and stolen private information. Cyber-criminals use social engineering to trick you into downloading malware off the internet or make you fill in your personal information under false pretences. A phishing scam in an email message can be evaded by keeping certain things in mind.

- Look for spelling mistakes in the text. Cyber criminals are not known for their grammar and spelling.
- Hover your cursor over the hyperlinked URL but don't click. Check if the address matches with the one written in the message.
- Watch out for fake threats. Did you receive a message saying "your email account will be closed if you don't reply to this email"? They might trick you by threatening that your security has been compromised.
- Attackers use the names and logos of well-known web sites to deceive you. The graphics and the web addresses used in the email are strikingly similar to the legitimate ones, but they lead you to phony sites.

Not all phishing is done via email or web sites. Vishing (Voice Phishing) involves calls to victims using fake identity fooling you into considering the call to be from a trusted organization. They may claim to be from a bank asking you to dial a number (provided by VoIP service and owned by attacker) and enter your account details. Once you do that, your account security is compromised.

Treat all unsolicited phone calls with scepticism and never provide any personal information. Many banks have issued pre-emptive warnings informing their users of phishing scams and the do's and don'ts regarding your account information.

IPC Section 379: Punishment for theft

Whoever commits theft shall be punished with imprisonment of either description for a term which may extend to three years, or with fine, or with both.

Classification of Offence:

Punishment - Imprisonment for 3 years, or fine, or both - Compoundable by the owner of the property stolen with the permission of the court

IPC Section 420: Cheating and dishonestly inducing delivery of property

Whoever cheats and thereby dishonestly induces the person deceived any property to any person, or to make, alter or destroy the whole or any part of a valuable security, or anything which is signed or sealed, and which is capable of being converted into a valuable security, shall be punished with imprisonment of either description for a term which may extend to seven years, and shall also be liable to fine.

Classification of Offence:

Punishment - Imprisonment for 7 years and fine - Compoundable by the person cheated with the permission of the court.

Section 66: Computer Related Offences

If any person, dishonestly, or fraudulently, does any act referred to in section 43, he shall be punishable with imprisonment for a term which may extend to two three years or with fine which may extend to five lakh rupees or with both.

Explanation: For the purpose of this section-

a) the word "dishonestly" shall have the meaning assigned to it in section 24 of the Indian Penal Code;

b) the word "fraudulently" shall have the meaning assigned to it in section 25 of the Indian Penal Code.

Section 66A: Punishment for sending offensive messages through communication service

Any person who sends, by means of a computer resource or a communication device,

a) any information that is grossly offensive or has menacing character; or

b) any information which he knows to be false, but for the purpose of causing annoyance, inconvenience, danger, obstruction, insult, injury, criminal intimidation, enmity, hatred, or ill will, persistently makes by making use of such computer resource or a communication device,

c) any electronic mail or electronic mail message for the purpose of causing annoyance or inconvenience or to deceive or to mislead the addressee or recipient about the origin of such messages shall be punishable with imprisonment for a term which may extend to two three years and with fine.

Explanation: For the purposes of this section, terms "Electronic Mail" and "Electronic Mail Message" means a message or information created or transmitted or received on a computer, computer system, computer resource or communication device including attachments in text, image, audio, video and any other electronic record, which may be transmitted with the message.

Section 66C: Punishment for identity theft

Whoever, fraudulently or dishonestly make use of the electronic signature, password or any other unique identification feature of any other person, shall be punished with imprisonment of either description for a term which may extend to three years and shall also be liable to fine which may extend to rupees one lakh.

Section 66D: Punishments for cheating by personation by using computer resource (IT Act 2000)

Whoever, by means of any communication device or computer resource cheats by personation, shall be punished with imprisonment of either description for a term which may extend to three years and shall also be liable to fine which may extend to one lakh rupees.

Illustration 1:

The 'Shipping Information' Phishing Scam: Internet security company Comodo disclosed a new type of phishing scam specifically targeting small businesses. Phishing emails were sent out to more than 3,000 businesses, including the subject line 'Shipping Information'. The email noted a forthcoming delivery by United Parcel Service (UPS) and included a seemingly innocent package tracking link. When the recipient clicked on the link it contained malware, potentially releasing a virus.

Illustration 2:

WannaCry: On May 12, 2017, WannaCry exploited a weakness in Microsoft's operating systems to deliberately infect computers. When the worm was infiltrated, it encrypted the infected operating systems, rendering them unusable. The hackers subsequently demanded a ransom for unlocking the encryption. Small businesses void of up-to-take IT infrastructure were particularly exposed to the WannaCry attack.

Illustration 3:

Petya Cyber-Attack: The Petya ransomware attack hit businesses, preventing victims from accessing their data until they paid $300 in BitCoins. The ransomware exploited vulnerabilities in Microsoft systems.

Shipping company Maersk was a victim of cybercrime and has said, following the attack, it has put "different and further protection measures" in place.

Illustration 4:

Shadow Brokers: Hacking group Shadow Brokers first surfaced in August 2016, but in April 2017 the group made its most impactful release yet. The attack comprised of a trove of alleged NSA tools, including a Windows exploit known as ExternalBlue. The Shadow Brokers leak has revitalized concerns of the dangers of using bugs in commercial products for intelligence-gathering.

Illustration 5:

IRS W2 Tax Season Spear-Phishing Scam: At the beginning of this year's tax season in the United States, a spear-phishing attack circulated. The W2 Phishing scam involved cyber criminals sending out fake emails. The hackers deliberately made the emails look like they were being sent from corporate executives.

The fake emails requested the personal information of employees for purposes related to tax and compliance. By the middle of March 2017, the phishing scam had compromised more than 120,000 employees at more than 100 different organizations.

Illustration 6:

Business Email Compromise (BEC): In 2017, the Nigeria-based Business Email Compromise (BEC) attack hit over 50 countries, targeting more than 500 businesses, predominantly industrial companies. The phishing scam prompted recipients to download a malicious file. When the file was downloaded, malware would gain authorized access to business data and networks.

Illustration 7:

Phishing Attack on Chipotle: In February 2017, a group of cyber criminals in Eastern Europe sent out emails laden with malware to staff of Chipotle. By clicking on the fake emails, the oblivious staff inadvertently enabled the hackers to compromise the POS systems of the majority of Chipotle locations. The hackers were then able to obtain the credit card data of millions of people.

Illustration 8:

Google Docs Hack: In May 2017, more than 3 million workers worldwide were forced to stop work when phishers sent out fraudulent emails invitations on Google docs inviting recipients to edit documents. When the recipients opened the invitations, they were taken to a third-party app, which enabled hackers to access individuals' Gmail accounts.

Illustration 9:

Phishing Attack on Qatar: In the first quarter of 2017, businesses in Qatar were targeted with tens of thousands of phishing attacks in just a three-month period. Qatar's phishing attacks involved the hackers sending out malicious emails and SMS texts to businesses, designed to compromise valuable information and data.

Illustration 10:

Amazon Prime Day Phishing Attack: Known as the Amazon Prime Day phishing attack, hackers are sending out seemingly legitimate deals to customers of Amazon. When Amazon's customers attempted to purchase the 'deals', the transaction would not be completed, promoting the retailer's customers to input data that could be compromised and stolen.

Illustration 11:

RBI Phishing Scam: In a daring phishing attack of its kind, the fraudsters even have not spared the Reserve Bank of India. The phishing email disguised as originating from the RBI, promised its recipient prize money of Rs.10 Lakhs within 48 hours, by giving a link which leads the user to a website that resembles the official website of RBI with the similar logo and web address. The user is then asked to reveal his personal information like password, I-pin number and savings account number. However, the RBI posted a warning regarding the fraudulent phishing e-mail on the bank's official website.

Data Theft and Source Code Theft

Data theft is a relatively new arena of crime in India. Owning to the sharp rise in use of Internet and technology, a new era of virtual reality has come up. The virtual world has created a new breed of criminals, who take advantage of the vulnerability of computer programs and use it for their personal gain or just to cause mischief. Such criminal elements need to be punished so that the society and the citizens can live without fear.

With the rise and growth of digital information and digital commerce, where our day to day lives are linked to the Internet, transactions based over emails and networking sites, e-shopping sites being the trend, where businesses are based in the virtual space and everything is digitized, data theft remains a huge threat to the people in general.

Under the Indian law, theft can only be committed in respect of movable property. Data is not a movable property, and hence the unauthorized act of taking away data electronically such as emailing it to oneself or by hacking into a computer system, is not considered as theft. However, stealing of data is no doubt a crime, and is punishable under the law.

What is the protection available?

- Under the Indian law, theft can only be committed in respect of movable property and data is not a movable property.

- No single law precisely deals with stealing of data but the act can be reported and punished under the umbrella of various other laws.

Definition of Data:

- A representation of information, knowledge, facts, concepts or instructions which are being prepared or have been prepared in a formalized manner.
- This information is either intended to processed, is being processed or has been processed.
- It can be in any form stored internally in a computer system or computer network.

Data is generally stolen:

- By employees or contractors using it in the course of their official work.
- Through hacking of computer systems.

In the former case, it is advisable that the agreements with the employees and contractors contain suitable provisions which can establish a breach of trust for unauthorised use and access of data. These agreements should clearly record that there is an entrustment of data to these parties and should restrict the scope and manner in which they may deal with the data. For example: If the employee in question has signed a Non-Disclosure Agreement with regard to a particular project and then misuses that information by giving it to someone else or using it for his/her benefit, then he/she can be held criminally liable for breaching the terms under the NDA and thereafter be heavily penalized for the same.

Preventive Measures / Precautions:

- Copyright your program code/software/data.

- Create a license agreement with your customers/users.
- Obfuscate your code.
- Provide a trial version of your code.
- Never share complete code/data required to run the software with a single person in your company.
- Never allow your employees to copy/share the data/ software on their personnel gadgets/emails/external drives and along with that make company devices secured to prevent data theft from the devices.
- Always assign specific duties to each employees.
- Always make non-disclosure agreement with the employees.
- Always make inventory of the hardware/software issued to employees.
- Train your employees and prepare them for phishing attempts and privacy breaches.
- Create user accounts for each employee to prevent unauthorized users from gaining access to your business computers. Laptops can be stolen easily; make sure they're locked when unattended.
- To prevent outsiders from gaining access to private information on your network, enable your operating system's firewall or purchase reputable firewall software.

Section 43(b):

(b) downloads, copies or extracts any data, computer data base or information from such computer, computer system or computer network including information or data held or stored in any removable storage medium;

Section 66: Computer Related Offences

If any person, dishonestly, or fraudulently, does any act referred to in section 43, he shall be punishable with imprisonment for a term which may extend to two three years or with fine which may extend to five lakh rupees or with both.

Section 43(j):

(j) steal, conceals, destroys or alters or causes any person to steal, conceal, destroy or alter any computer source code used for a computer resource with an intention to cause damage; he shall be liable to pay damages by way of compensation to the person so affected.

Explanation: For the purposes of this section,-

(i) "computer contaminant" means any set of computer instructions that are designed-

(a) to modify, destroy, record, transmit data or programme residing within a computer, computer system or computer network; or

(b) by any means to usurp the normal operation of the computer, computer system, or computer network;

(ii) "computer database" means a representation of information, knowledge, facts, concepts or instructions in text, image, audio, video that are being prepared or have been prepared in a formalised manner or have been produced by a computer, computer system or computer network and are intended for use in a computer, computer system or computer network;

(iii) "computer virus" means any computer instruction, information, data or programme that destroys, damages, degrades or adversely affects the performance of a computer resource or attaches itself to another computer resource and operates when a programme, data or instruction is executed or some other event takes place in that computer resource;

(iv) "damage" means to destroy, alter, delete, add, modify or rearrange any computer resource by any means;

(v) "computer source code" means the listing of programmes, computer commands, design and layout and programme analysis of computer resource in any form.

Section 65: Tampering with Computer Source Documents

If any person knowingly or intentionally conceals, destroys code or alters or causes another to conceal, destroy code or alter any computer, computer program, computer system, or computer network he shall be punishable with imprisonment up to three years, or with fine up to two lakh rupees, or with both.

Section 66B: Punishment for dishonestly receiving stolen computer resource or communication device

Whoever dishonestly receives or retains any stolen computer resource or communication device knowing or having reason to believe the same to be stolen computer resource or communication device shall be punished with imprisonment of either description for a term which may extend to three years or with fine which may extend to rupees one lakh or with both.

IPC Section 379: Punishment for theft

Whoever commits theft shall be punished with imprisonment of either description for a term which may extend to three years, or with fine, or with both.

Classification of Offence:

Punishment - Imprisonment for 3 years, or fine, or both - Compoundable by the owner of the property stolen with the permission of the court

IPC Section 405: Criminal breach of trust

Whoever, being in any manner entrusted with property, or with any dominion over property, dishonestly misappropriates or converts to his own use that property, or dishonestly uses or disposes of that property in violation of any direction of law prescribing the mode in which such trust is to be discharged, or of any legal contract, express or implied, which he has made touching the discharge of such trust, or willfully suffers any other person so to do, commits "criminal breach of trust".

IPC Section 420: Cheating and dishonestly inducing delivery of property

Whoever cheats and thereby dishonestly induces the person deceived any property to any person, or to make, alter or destroy the whole or any part of a valuable security, or anything which is signed or sealed, and which is capable of being converted into a valuable security, shall be punished with imprisonment of either description for a term which may extend to seven years, and shall also be liable to fine.

Classification of Offence:

Punishment - Imprisonment for 7 years and fine - Compoundable by the person cheated with the permission of the court.

Section 63: Offence of infringement of copyright or other rights conferred by this Act

Any person who knowingly infringes or abets the infringement of

(a) the copyright in a work, or

(b) any other right conferred by this Act, [except the right conferred by section 53A] [shall be punishable with imprisonment for a term which shall not be less than six months but which may extend to three years and with fine which shall not be less than fifty thousand rupees but which may extend to two lakh rupees: Provided that [where the infringement has not been made for gain in the course of trade or business] the court may, for adequate and special reasons to be mentioned in the judgment, impose a sentence of imprisonment for a term of less than six months or a fine of less than fifty thousand rupees.]

Explanation: Construction of a building or other structure which infringes or which, if completed, would infringe the copyright in some other work shall not be an offence under this section.

Illustration 1:

Just Dial, with a single national number 69999999 in 240 cities, has obtained injunction against Infomedia 18 Limited (one of the group company of media group TV 18), restraining it from carrying out any business or rendering any service of providing information of business, services, and products, through their newly launched website askme.in

In a suit filed by Just Dial against Infomedia 18, Just Dial alleged that Infomedia 18 had copied its extensive database and was displaying the same on its website askme.in, thereby infringing Just Dial's copyright in its valuable database. The Delhi High Court has granted an exparte injunction against Infomedia 18, restraining them from infringing Just Dial's copyright and from running the website askme.in till the next date of hearing. The High Court has also appointed commissioners to visit Infomedia 18 Ltd's office in Delhi and Mumbai and to seize and take into custody all the CPUs, compact, floppy discs and/ or other storage media containing any part of the commercial or business directory database belonging to Just Dial.

Illustration 2:

The Chester Crown Court has ordered two former employees of UK mobile operator T-Mobile to pay a total of £73,700 after stealing and selling customer data from the company in 2008. It is a landmark ruling because, it is a record fine for data protection offences, but more important than that, is that for the very first time we are seeing the criminal courts taking data protection seriously, David Turley and Darren Hames pleaded guilty to offences under Section 55 of the Data Protection Act, but the fines were, imposed under the Proceeds of Crime Act. Mr. Turley was ordered to pay £45,000 and Mr. Hames was ordered to pay £28,700. Both face an 18-month prison term if they fail to pay within six months.

Ransomware and Cyber Extortion

Ransom, which refers to some kind of payment that is demanded in exchange for the release of someone or something that has been taken, is a simple yet effective ploy that has been used by criminals for thousands of years.

For example, on his way home from the Third Crusade in 1192, King Richard the Lionheart was captured and held for ransom by Duke Leopold of Austria. The amount demanded was so large that it took over a year for England to raise it, giving root to the now-familiar idiom "a king's ransom."

In 1932, the 20-month-old son of famous aviator Charles Lindbergh was kidnapped and held for ransom in one of the most high-profile cases in the history of the FBI.

The dynamics of ransom are not difficult to understand: "I take something dear to you, and you pay me to give it back."

Ancient Approaches, Modern Applications:

Today, criminals are applying these ancient approaches to modern technologies. Ransomware, one of the fastest -growing areas of cybercrime, refers to malicious software that is specifically designed to take control of a computer system or its data and hold it hostage so the attackers can demand payment from their victims. Although ransomware initially targeted PCs, it is now migrating to mobile platforms as well.

Some recent public disclosures involving demands for ransom include, but not limited to:

Illustration 1:

The town of Greenland, New Hampshire, which lost eight years' worth of data when it fell victim to a ransomware known as CryptoLocker.

Illustration 2:

Brokerage and investment advisory firm Benjamin F. Edwards, which exposed data related to some 430 New Hampshire residents from a ransomware called CryptoWall.

Illustration 3:

Domino's Pizza in France and Belgium where the personal information (including favorite pizza toppings) of about 650,000 customers was compromised. The hackers responsible demanded a ransom of 30,000 euros in exchange for not disclosing the information publicly.

Cyber Extortion: Related to Ransomware:

Note that, technically, this last example is not ransomware (a type of malicious software), but rather a demand for ransom for compromised customer data. It seems that criminals continue to move faster than the tech industry's ability to create new jargon to describe it. In practical terms, it shows that we should also be aware of another ancient and effective exploit: extortion, which is the crime of taking money (or something else of value) from another party by use of threat or force.

The dynamics of extortion are not difficult to understand, either: "I cause (or threaten to cause) you harm, and you pay me to stop."

Public disclosures related to cyber extortion, however not limited to:

Illustration 1:

News aggregator Feedly was the victim of a distributed denial-of-service (DDoS) attack in which the attackers demanded payment to make it stop.

Illustration 2:

Move Inc., an online real estate services provider, battled DDoS attacks that disrupted its website operations. It refused to respond to a demand for payment.

Illustration 3:

Evernote also battled a DDoS attack that disrupted operations, although it is unclear in this case whether the attackers also demanded payment.

Although these particular examples of cyber extortion are against larger-scale targets, it's worth noting that the tactic can also be directed at smaller, personal targets — no one is really immune.

What You Need to Do

To protect against ransomware, now is the perfect time for organizations to remind themselves of some basic best practices:

- Back up your data regularly (from an end user's perspective, this is the easiest way out).
- Ensure that your endpoints and servers are patched and up-to-date.
- Deploy appropriate endpoint protection.
- Regularly make end users aware of safe email and Web-browsing practices, and periodically test their behavior.

To protect against cyber extortion, it is essential for all organizations to understand the importance of developing a strong incident response capability to complement their traditional prevention-oriented security strategies. Prevention cannot be successful 100% of the time, so it makes sense to be capable of detecting and responding to incidents more quickly when they do occur. Note that incident response is not an action that an organization needs at a specific point in time; rather, it is a capability that an organization develops and uses when needed.

Section 66 and 43(e) of the I.T. Act covers the offence of ransomware and cyber extortion.

Section 66: Computer Related Offences

If any person, dishonestly, or fraudulently, does any act referred to in section 43, he shall be punishable with imprisonment for a term which may extend to two three years or with fine which may extend to five lakh rupees or with both.

Explanation: For the purpose of this section-

a) the word "dishonestly" shall have the meaning assigned to it in section 24 of the Indian Penal Code;

b) the word "fraudulently" shall have the meaning assigned to it in section 25 of the Indian Penal Code.

Section 43(e): If any person without permission of the owner or any other person who is in-charge of a computer, computer system or computer network - disrupts or causes disruption of any computer, computer system or computer network;

he shall be liable to pay damages by way of compensation not exceeding one crore rupees to the person so affected. (Change vide ITAA 2008)

Section 384: Punishment for extortion

Whoever commits extortion shall be punished with imprisonment of either description for a term which may extend to three years, or with fine or with both.

Credit Card Frauds and Online Banking Frauds

Online fraud is one of the most widespread forms of cybercrime. As more and more people use their phones and computers for banking and online shopping, they become more attractive to cybercriminals, who use email messages, website, chat rooms, message boards and social networks to get access to your personal information.

In order to protect yourself against this type of crime, it is important to recognize the different types of scams criminals are using. These include:

- **Key loggers:** These devices log all the keystrokes entered on a particular computer. The keystrokes are then retrieved by criminals and used for their own purposes. The key logger could be hidden in an email attachment sent to you, or the criminal can install it when working on your computer via a memory stick.
- **Phishing:** Fraudsters send you an email that looks like it is from a reputable institution such as your bank. You are asked to click on a link in the email or on the attachment which opens a fake website which looks exactly like the real thing. You are then asked to enter personal details such as your PIN, password, bank account or credit card details. Once all the sensitive information is obtained, they use it to defraud you.

- **SMShing:** This cousin of phishing uses text messages on cellphones and smartphones instead of e-mails. The message is usually about something urgent, for example your credit card has been stolen, and instructs you to go to a certain Web site or call a phone number to verify your account information. The thieves on the receiving end then use your information to steal money from your account or open new credit cards in your name.
- **Deposit refund scam:** This is where criminals contact you to tell you that an amount of money was 'mistakenly' deposited into your account. The caller will ask you to refund the amount and will fax a 'proof of payment' to you. After you have refunded the money electronically, you will never see it again once the bank reverses the fraudulent deposit.
- **Vishing:** The criminal practice of using social engineering over the telephone system to gain access to private personal and financial information from the public for the purpose of financial reward. The word that is a combination of "voice" and "phishing".

In such matters, the complainant alleges that some unknown person had withdrawn money/made transactions through his/her credit/debit cards through online purchasing. In most of these cases purchasing is done by using following crucial information of the credit/debit card:

- The 16 Digit Credit/Debit Card Number
- The validity of the Credit/Debit card
- The 3 digit confidential Card Verification Value (CVV) or the One-Time-Password (OTP) sent on the registered mobile number of the Debit Card holder.

While it may be that the Card Number and the validity of the card is made available to the fraudsters through insider in the bank, the OTP is procured by them by deceiving the account holder to share the OTP on the pretext that it is required for account verification, etc.

Preventive Measures / Precautions

- Don't give your account number to anyone on the phone unless you've made the call to a company you know to be reputable. If you've never done business with them before, do an online search first for reviews or complaints.
- During a transaction, keep your eye on your card. Make sure you get it back before you walk away.
- Monitor your bank and credit card statements.
- Monitor your credit report.
- Never store Credit Card information online.
- Never make use of Credit Card on Public Computer.

Do's

- Put your signature on the card immediately upon its receipt
- Make the photocopy of both the sides of your card and preserve it at a safe place to remember the card number, expiration date in case of loss of card
- Change the default personal identification number (PIN) received from the bank before doing any transaction
- Always carry the details about contact numbers of your bank in case of loss of your card
- Carry your cards in a separate pouch / card holder than your wallet
- Keep an eye on your card during the transaction, and ensure to get it back immediately

- Preserve all the receipts to compare with credit card invoice
- Reconcile your monthly invoice/statement with your receipts
- Report immediately any discrepancy observed in the monthly invoice/statement
- Destroy all the receipts after reconciling it with the monthly invoice/statement
- Inform your bank in advance, about any change in your contact details such as home address, phone number and e-mail address
- Ensure the legitimacy of the website before providing any of your card details
- Report the loss of the card immediately in your bank and at the police station, if necessary

Dont's

- Store your card number and PINs in your cell
- Lend your cards to anyone
- Leave cards or transaction receipts lying around
- Sign a blank receipt (if the transaction details are not legible, ask for another receipt to ensure the amount instead of trusting the seller)
- Write your card number/PIN on a postcard or the outside of an envelope
- Give out immediately your account number over the phone (unless you are calling to a company / to your bank)
- Destroy credit card receipts by simply dropping into garbage box/dustbin

Section 66C: Punishment for identity theft

Whoever, fraudulently or dishonestly make use of the electronic signature, password or any other unique identification feature of any other person, shall be punished with imprisonment of either description for a term which may extend to three years and shall also be liable to fine which may extend to rupees one lakh.

Section 66: Computer Related Offences

If any person, dishonestly, or fraudulently, does any act referred to in section 43, he shall be punishable with imprisonment for a term which may extend to two three years or with fine which may extend to five lakh rupees or with both.

Explanation: For the purpose of this section-

a) the word "dishonestly" shall have the meaning assigned to it in section 24 of the Indian Penal Code;

b) the word "fraudulently" shall have the meaning assigned to it in section 25 of the Indian Penal Code.

Section 43 of ITA 2008 case will be filled.

Section 43: Penalty and Compensation for damage to computer, computer system

If any person without permission of the owner or any other person who is in-charge of a computer, computer system or computer network -

(a) accesses or secures access to such computer, computer system or computer network or computer resource

(b) downloads, copies or extracts any data, computer data base or information from such computer, computer system or computer network including information or data held or stored in any removable storage medium;

(c) introduces or causes to be introduced any computer contaminant or computer virus into any computer, computer system or computer network;

(d) damages or causes to be damaged any computer, computer system or computer network, data, computer data base or any other programmes residing in such computer, computer system or computer network;

(e) disrupts or causes disruption of any computer, computer system or computer network;

(f) denies or causes the denial of access to any person authorised to access any computer, computer system or computer network by any means;

(g) provides any assistance to any person to facilitate access to a computer, computer system or computer network in contravention of the provisions of this Act, rules or regulations made thereunder,

(h) charges the services availed of by a person to the account of another person by tampering with or manipulating any computer, computer system, or computer network,

(i) destroys, deletes or alters any information residing in a computer resource or diminishes its value or utility or affects it injuriously by any means

(ii) Steals, conceals, destroys or alters or causes any person to steal, conceal, destroy or alter any computer source code used for a computer resource with an intention to cause damage, he shall be liable to pay damages by way of compensation not exceeding one crore rupees to the person so affected. (Change vide ITAA 2008)

Illustration

Court of Metropolitan Magistrate Delhi found guilty a 24-year-old engineer working in a call centre, of fraudulently gaining the details of Campa's credit card and bought a television and a cordless phone from Sony website. Metropolitan magistrate Gulshan Kumar convicted Azim for cheating under 418, 419, 420 sections of the IPC, but did not send him to jail. Instead, Azim was asked to furnish a personal bond of Rs. 20,000, and was released on a year's probation.

Illustration

Well known actor and director Amol Palekar, was at the receiving end of a credit card fraud as an unknown person(s) used his credit card details to book a couple of air tickets online. The card was issued by Bank of India, Mumbai, and Palekar was faced with a bill of around Rs. 60K for this transaction.

Illustration

Almost 30 customers of Hotel Le Meridien, Pune were cheated. Four persons were creating duplicate credit cards from those belonging to customers and then using them to make purchases. One of the personnel was a cashier at the Chingari Restaurant in Hotel Le Meridien, and he used credit card skimmers and readers which recorded details of the credit card being swiped. These details were then copied on blank cards with magnetic strips. Altogether they used 33 cards of 27 banks among themselves to go on a shopping spree, with the total amount of such purchases being pegged at Rs. 1 crore. The type of cards being targeted were the higher end ones, namely, Gold, Titanuim, Platinum and corporate cards, where the credit limit was higher. This came to light when a Citibank employee went to the hotel with some friends and lodged a police complaint after getting his card bill with exorbitant purchases that he had no idea about.

Electronic / Digital Signatures

Digital Signature:

A digital signature is a technique to validate the legitimacy of a digital message or a document. A valid digital signature provides the surety to the recipient that the message was generated by a known sender, such that the sender cannot deny having sent the message. Digital signatures are mostly used for software distribution, financial transactions, and in other cases where there is a risk of forgery.

Electronic Signature:

An electronic signature or e-signature indicates either that a person who demands to have created a message is the one who created it.

A signature can be defined as a schematic script related with a person. A signature on a document is a sign that the person accepts the purposes recorded in the document. In many engineering companies digital seals are also required for another layer of authentication and security. Digital seals and signatures are same as handwritten signatures and stamped seals.

Digital Signature to Electronic Signature:

Digital Signature was the term defined in the old I.T.Act, 2000. Electronic Signature is the term defined by the amended act (I.T. Act, 2008). The concept of Electronic Signature is broader than Digital Signature. Section 3 of the Act delivers for the verification of Electronic Records by affixing Digital Signature.

As per the amendment, verification of electronic record by electronic signature or electronic authentication technique shall be considered reliable.

According to the United Nations Commission on International Trade Law (UNCITRAL), electronic authentication and signature methods may be classified into the following categories:

- Those based on the knowledge of the user or the recipient, i.e., passwords, personal identification numbers (PINs), etc.
- Those based on the physical features of the user, i.e., biometrics.
- Those based on the possession of an object by the user, i.e., codes or other information stored on a magnetic card.
- Types of authentication and signature methods that, without falling under any of the above categories might also be used to indicate the originator of an electronic communication (Such as a facsimile of a handwritten signature, or a name typed at the bottom of an electronic message).

According to the UNCITRAL MODEL LAW on Electronic Signatures, the following technologies are presently in use:

- Digital Signature within a public key infrastructure (PKI)
- Biometric Device
- PINs

- Passwords
- Scanned handwritten signature
- Signature by Digital Pen
- Clickable "OK" or "I Accept" or "I Agree" click boxes

According to section 71 of the IT Act

Whoever makes any misrepresentation to, or suppresses any material fact from, the Controller or the Certifying Authority for obtaining any licence or Digital Signature Certificate, as the case may be, shall be punished with imprisonment for a term which may extend to two years, or with fine which may extend to one lakh rupees, or with both.

This section applies to:

1. a person, who, for obtaining a digital signature certificate-
    a. makes a misrepresentation to the Certifying Authority,
    b. suppresses any material fact from the Certifying Authority.
2. a person obtaining a license to operate as a Certifying Authority –
    a. makes a misrepresentation to the Controller,
    b. suppresses any material fact from the Controller.

Let us examine the essential terms of this section.

Misrepresentation implies "presenting information incorrectly, improperly or falsely". There must be a deliberate intention to deceive.

Illustration

Ram is applying for a digital signature certificate. He fills in his name as "Krishna" and also submits photocopies of Krishna's passport as proof of identity. Ram is liable for misrepresenting information to the Certifying Authority. Suppress implies "to withhold from disclosure".

Illustration

Noodle Ltd is applying for a licence to become a Certifying Authority. One of the questions in the application form is "In case any of the company directors been convicted for a criminal offence, then please mention relevant details."

One of the Noodle directors has been convicted in the past. But, Noodle officials submit the filled in form with the answer to this question being left blank.

The officials will be liable for suppressing information from the Controller.

Material fact implies something that is relevant, pertinent or essential. The punishment provided is imprisonment up to 2 years and / or fine up to Rs 1 lakh.

False Certificates

According to section 73 of the IT Act

(1) No person shall publish a Digital Signature Certificate or otherwise make it available to any other person with the knowledge that—

> (a) the Certifying Authority listed in the certificate has not issued it; or

(b) the subscriber listed in the certificate has not accepted it; or

(c) the certificate has been revoked or suspended, unless such publication is for the purpose of verifying a digital signature created prior to such suspension or revocation.

(2) Any person who contravenes the provisions of sub-section

(1) shall be punished with imprisonment for a term which may extend to two years, or with fine which may extend to one lakh rupees, or with both.

Illustration 1

Ram has created a fake digital signature certificate purporting to have been issued by Noodle Certifying Authority. Ram plans to use this certificate to carry out some financial frauds. He posts this certificate on his website. He is liable under this section.

Illustration 2

Rekha has applied to Noodle Certifying Authority for a digital signature certificate. Noodle in due course issues the certificate to Rekha. She however does not accept it as some of the details are incorrect in the certificate. In the meanwhile Noodle Ltd publishes her certificate in their online repository. In this case Noodle Ltd will be liable under this section.

Illustration 3

Rekha is employed with Noodle Ltd. She has obtained a digital signature certificate for official purposes on 1st January. She quits her job on 1st June and her certificate is revoked on that day. Noodle Ltd continues to keep Rekha's revoked certificate in its online repository even after 1st June. Noodle Ltd will be liable under this section. They will not be liable if the purpose behind keeping Rekha's certificate in their repository is to verify documents signed by Rekha between 1st January and 1st June. The punishment provided for this section is imprisonment up to 2 years and / or fine up to Rs 1 lakh.

Fraudulent Use

According to section 74 of the IT Act

Whoever knowingly creates; publishes or otherwise makes available a Digital Signature Certificate for any fraudulent or unlawful purpose shall be punished with imprisonment for a term which may extend to two years, or with fine which may extend to one lakh rupees, or with both.

Creating a digital signature certificate is technologically not a very difficult task. All that is needed is a computer running the Windows 2003 Server operating system and having Certificate Services installed. This makes it easy for criminals to create and publish digital signature certificates for fraudulent and unlawful purposes. Let us examine some of the terms used in this section.

Creates means "to bring into existence"

Illustration

Ram has a computer running the Windows 2003 Server operating system and having Certificate Services installed. He uses this computer to generate a digital signature certificate for himself and Rekha. He has created the said certificates.

Publishes means "to make known to others"

Illustration

Ram uploads Rekha's digital signature certificate onto a publicly accessible part of his website. He has published her certificate.

The concept of make available can be explained using a simple illustration.

Illustration

Ram has a computer running the Windows 2003 Server operating system and having Certificate Services installed. He uses this computer to generate a digital signature certificate in Rekha's name. He then gives this certificate to Krishna who plans to misuse it to spoof Rekha's emails. Here Ram has made the certificate available to Krishna for an unlawful purpose.

Illustration

Mr. Deshpande publishes his Electronic Signature but the issuing certifying authority (CA), which is shown on his Electronic Certificate, does not confirm issuance of the said certificate because Mr. Deshpande has faked CA's name on the electronic certificate. This act of Mr. Deshpande is a cyber crime.

Illustration

Mr. Tiwari enters into a transaction of E-Contract with an USA based software company. He signs this contract with the Electronic Signature which was revoked by the Certifying Authority and which is no longer valid. The act of Mr. Tiwari knowingly signing using revoked or suspended certificate is a cyber crime.

Various Types of Cyber Crimes

Cyber Crime against Person:

- **Harassment via E-mails:** It is a very common type of harassment done through letters, attachments of files & folders i.e. via e-mails. At present, harassment is common with the increase in the usage of social networking sites, like Facebook, Twitter etc.

- **Cyber Stalking:** It means expressed or implied physical threat that creates fear through the use of computer technology such as internet, e-mail, phones, text messagaes, webcam, websites or video.

- **Dissemination of Obscene Material:** It includes Indecent exposure / Pornography (basically child pornography), hosting of website containing these prohibited materials. These obscene matters may cause harm to the mind of the adolescent and tend to deprave or corrupt their mind.

- **Malware:** Malware is software that takes control of any individual's computer to spread a bug to other people's devices or social networking profiles. Such software can also be used to create a 'botnet' - a network of computers controlled remotely by hackers, known as 'herders,' - to spread spam or viruses.

- **Defamation:** It is an act of imputing any person with intent to lower down the dignity of the person by hacking his mail account and sending some mails with vulgar language to unknown persons mail account.

- **Hacking:** It means unauthorized control / access over computer system and act of hacking completely destroys the whole data as well as computer programmes. Hackers usually hack telecommunication and mobile network.

- **Cracking:** It is amongst the gravest cyber crimes known till date. It is a dreadful feeling to know that a stranger has broken into your computer systems without your knowledge and consent and has tampered with precious confidential data and information.

- **E-Mail Spoofing**: A spoofed e-mail may be said to be one, which misrepresents its origin. It shows its origin to be different from which actually it originates.

- **SMS Spoofing:** Spoofing is a blocking through spam which means the unwanted uninvited messages. Here a offender steals identity of another in the form of mobile phone number and sending SMS via internet and receiver gets the SMS from the mobile phone number of the victim. It is a very serious cyber crime against any individual.

- **Carding:** It means false ATM cards, i.e., Debit and Credit cards used by criminals for their monetary benefits through withdrawing money from the victim's bank account malafidely. There is always unauthorized use of ATM cards in this type of cyber crimes.

- **Cheating & Fraud:** It means the person who is doing the act of cyber crime i.e. stealing password and data storage has done it with wrongful intention which leads to fraud and cheating.

- **Child Pornography:** It involves the use of computer networks to create, distribute, or access materials that sexually exploit underage children.

- **Phishing:** Phishing is just one of the many frauds on the Internet. Phishing trying to fool people into parting with their money. Phishing refers to the receipt of unsolicited e-mails by customers of financial institutions, requesting them to enter their username, password or other personal information to access their account for some reason. Customers are directed to a fraudulent replica of the original institution's website when they click on the links on the email to enter their information, and so they remain unaware that the fraud has occurred. The fraudster then has access to the customer's online bank account and to the funds contained in that account.

  The above fraud message is a classic example of a phishing scam. This is how fraudsters operate. The full site address is same except "s" missing in "https" and small letter "L" used instead of " i" as in ICICI. It looks similar to ICICI banks Web address. You may receive similar messages from fraudsters. Please DO NOT click on such links.

- **Vishing:** Vishing is the criminal practice of using social engineering and Voice over IP (VoIP) to gain access to private personal and financial information from the public for the purpose of financial reward. The term is a combination of "voice" and "phishing".

- **Bot Networks:** A cyber crime called 'Bot Networks', wherein spamsters and other perpetrators of cyber crimes remotely take control of computers without the users realizing it, is increasing at an alarming rate. Computers get linked to Bot Networks when users unknowingly download malicious codes such as Trojan horse sent as e-mail attachments. Such affected computers, known as zombies, can work together whenever the malicious code within them get activated, and those who are behind the Bot Networks attacks get the computing powers of thousands of systems at their disposal. Attackers often coordinate large groups of Botcontrolled systems, or Boot networks, to scan for vulnerable systems and use them to increase the speed and breadth of their attacks. Boot networks create unique problems for organizations because they can be remotely upgraded with new exploits very quickly and this could help attackers pre-empt security efforts.

- **Assault by Threat:** It refers to threatening a person with fear for their lives or lives of their families through the use of a computer network i.e., E-mail, videos or phones.

- **Buffer Overflow:** This is the most common way ofbreaking into a computer. Buffers are created to hold a finite amount of data. When it overflows, it goes into adjacent buffers which can cause data to be overwritten. In buffer overflow attacks, the extra data can contain instructions that trigger specific actions. These actions can cause damage to files and / or change data.

Cyber Crime against Person's Property

- **Intellectual Property Crimes:** Intellectual property

consists of a bundle of rights. Any unlawful act by which the owner is deprived completely or partially of his rights is an offence. The common form of IPR violation may be said to be software piracy, infringement of copyright, trademark, patents, designs and service mark violation, theft of computer source code, etc.

- **Software Piracy:** Many people do not consider software piracy to be theft. They would never steal a rupee from someone but would not think twice before using pirated software. There is a common perception amongst normal computer users to not consider software as "property". This has led the software piracy to become a flourishing business.

  The software pirate sells the pirated software in physical media (usually CD ROMs) through a close network of dealers.

  The suspect uses high speed CD duplication equipment to create multiple copies of the pirated software. This software is sold through a network of computer hardware and software vendors.

- **Cyber Squatting::** It means where two persons claim for the same Domain Name either by claiming that they had registered the name first on by right of using it before the other or using something similar to that previously.

  For example, two similar names, i.e., www.yahoo.com and www.yaahoo.com.

- **Cyber Vandalism:** Vandalism means deliberately destroying or damaging property of another. Thus cyber vandalism means destroying or damaging the data when a network service is stopped or disrupted. It may include within its purview any kind of physical harm done to the computer of any person. These acts may take the form of the theft of a computer, some part of a computer or a peripheral attached to the computer.

- **Hacking Computer System:** Hacktivism attacks those included Famous Twitter, blogging platform by unauthorized access/control over the computer. Due to the hacking activity there will be loss of data as well as computer. Also research especially indicates that those attacks were not mainly intended for financial gain too and to diminish the reputation of particular person or company.

  A hacker is an unauthorized user who attempts to or gains access to an information system. Hacking is a crime even if there is no visible damage to the system, since it is an invasion into the privacy of data.

- **Transmitting Virus:** Viruses are programs that attach themselves to a computer or a file and then circulate themselves to other files and to other computers on a network. They usually affect the data on a computer, either by altering or deleting it. Worm attacks plays major role in affecting the computerize system of the individuals.

- **Packet Sniffing:** This is used by hackers and forensic experts. Data travels in the form of packets and vary in size depending on the network bandwidth and amount of data. The hacker intercepts the transmission between computer A and B. All the hacker needs is the IP address from one of the computers and any data can be stolen. The data is not stolen because sniffers don't do that. Instead they copy the hex and translate it into original data. This is why it is hard for firewalls to detect this because they only provide application level security.

- **Cyber Tresspass:** It means to access someone's computer without the right authorization of the owner and does not disturb, alter, misuse, or damage data or system by using wireless internet connection.

- **Salami Attack:** Those attacks are used for the commission of financial crimes. The key here is to make the alteration so insignificant that in a single case it would go completely unnoticed. e.g., a bank employee inserts a program into bank's servers that deducts a small amount from the account of every customer

- **Internet Time Thefts:** Basically, Internet Time Theft comes under hacking. It is the use by an unauthorised person, of the Internet hours paid for by another person. The person who gets access to someone else's ISP user ID and password, either by hacking or by gaining access to it by illegal means, uses it to access the Internet without the other person's knowledge. You can identify time theft if your Internet time has to be recharged of ten, despite infrequent usage.

- **Trojan and Rats:** Trojan horses are programs that appear to be doing what the user wants while they are actually doing something else such as deleting files or formatting disks. All the user sees is the interface of the program that he wants to run. RATs are Remote Access Trojans that provide a backdoor into the system through which a hacker can snoop into your system and run malicious code.

- **Data Diddling:** Data Diddling involves changing data prior or during input into a computer. In other words, information is changed from the way it should be entered by a person typing in the data, a virus that changes data, the programmer of the database or application, or anyone else involved in the process of having information stored in a computer file. The culprit can be anyone involved in the process of creating, recording, encoding, examining, checking, converting, or transmitting data. This is one of the simplest methods of committing a computer-related crime, because it requires almost no computer skills whatsoever. Despite the ease of committing the crime, the cost can be considerable.

- **E-mail Account Hacking:** Emails are increasingly being used for social interaction, business communication and online transactions. Most email account holders do not take basic precautions to protect their email account passwords. Cases of theft of e-mail passwords and subsequent misuse of email accounts are becoming very common. The victim's e-mail account password is stolen and the account is then misused for sending out malicious code (virus, worm, Trojan etc) to people in the victim's address book. The recipients of these viruses believe that the e-mail is coming from a known person and run the attachments. This infects their computers with the malicious code.

The suspect would install key loggers in public computers (such as cyber cafes, airport lounges etc.) or the computers of the victim.

Cyber Crime against Government

- **Cyber Terroism:** Cyber terrorism is a major burning issue in the domestic as well as global concern. The common form of these terrorist attacks on the Internet is by distributed denial of service attacks, hate websites and hate e-mails, attacks on sensitive computer networks etc. Cyber terrorism activities endanger the sovereignty and integrity of the nation.

- **Web Defacement:** Website defacement is usually the substitution of the original home page of a website with another page (usually pornographic or defamatory in nature) by a hacker. Religious and government sites are regularly targeted by hackers in order to display political or religious beliefs. Under the scenario, the homepage of a website is replaced with a pornographic or defamatory page. In case of Government websites, this is most commonly done on symbolic days (e.g., the Independence Day of the country).

  The defacer may exploit the vulnerabilities of the operating system or applications used to host the website. This will allow him to hack into the web server and change the home page and other pages. Alternatively he may launch a brute force or dictionary attack to obtain the administrator passwords for the website. He can then connect to the web server and change the WebPages.

- **Cyber Warfare:** It refers to politically motivated hacking to conduct sabotage and espionage. It is a form of information warfare sometimes seen as analogous to conventional warfare although this analogy is controversial for both its accuracy and its political motivation.

- **Use of Internet and Computers by terrorists:** Many terrorists are using virtual as well as physical storage media for hiding information and records of their illicit business. They also use emails and chat rooms to communicate with their counterparts around the globe. The suspects carry laptops wherein information relating to their activities is stored in encrypted and password protected form. They also create email accounts using fictitious details. In many cases, one email account is shared by many people. E.g., one terrorist composes an e-mail and saves it in the draft folder. Another terrorist logs into the same account from another city / country and reads the saved email. He then composes his reply and saves it in the draft folder. The emails are not actually sent. This makes e-mail tracking and tracing almost impossible. For committing this crime the terrorists purchase small storage devices with large data storage capacities. They also purchase and use encryption software. The terrorists may also use free or paid accounts with online storage providers.

- **Distribution of pirated software:** It means distributing pirated software from one computer to another intending to destroy the data and official records of the government.

- **Possession of unauthorized information:** It is very easy to access any information by the terrorists with the aid of internet and to possess that information for political, religious, social, ideological objectives.

Cyber Crime against Society at large

- **Child Pornography:** It involves the use of computer networks to create, distribute, or access materials that sexually exploit underage children. It also includes activities concerning indecent exposure and obscenity.

- **Cyber Trafficking**: It may be trafficking in drugs, human beings, arms weapons etc. which affects large number of persons. Trafficking in the cyberspace is also a gravest crime.

- **Online Gambling:** Online fraud and cheating is one of the most lucrative businesses that are growing today in the cyber space. There are many cases that have come to light are those pertaining to credit card crimes, contractual crimes, offering jobs, etc.

- **Financial Crimes:** This type of offence is common as there is rapid growth in the users of networking sites and phone networking where culprit will try to attack by sending bogus mails or messages through internet. For example: Using credit cards by obtaining password illegally.

- **Forgery:** It means to deceive large number of persons by sending threatening mails as online business transactions are becoming the habitual need of today's lifestyle.

IT Act, 2000 – A Bird's Eye View

The Government of India enacted its Information Technology Act 2000 with the objectives stating officially as:

"to provide legal recognition for transactions carried out by means of electronic data interchange and other means of electronic communication, commonly referred to as "electronic commerce", which involve the use of alternatives to paper-based methods of communication and storage of information, to facilitate electronic filing of documents with the Government agencies and further to amend the Indian Penal Code, the Indian Evidence Act, 1872, the Bankers' Books Evidence Act, 1891 and the Reserve Bank of India Act, 1934 and for matters connected therewith or incidental thereto."

IT Act 2000 legislation deals with:

- Legal Recognition of Electronic Documents
- Legal Recognition of Digital Signatures
- Offenses and Contraventions

Why did the need for IT Amendment Act 2008 (ITAA) arise?

The IT Act 2000, being the first legislation on technology, computers, e-commerce and e-communication, there was the subject of extensive debates, elaborate reviews with one arm of the industry criticizing some sections of the Act to be draconian and other stating it is too diluted and lenient. There were some obvious omissions too resulting in the investigators relying more and more on the time-tested (one and half century-old) Indian Penal Code even in technology based cases with the IT Act also being referred in the process with the reliance more on IPC rather on the ITA.

Thus the need for an amendment – a detailed one – was felt for the I.T. Act. Major industry bodies were consulted and advisory groups were formed to go into the perceived lacunae in the I.T. Act and comparing it with similar legislations in other nations and to suggest recommendations. Such recommendations were analyzed and subsequently taken up as a comprehensive Amendment Act and after considerable administrative procedures; the consolidated amendment called the Information Technology Amendment Act 2008 was placed in the Parliament and passed at the end of 2008 (just after Mumbai terrorist attack of 26 November 2008 had taken place). The IT Amendment Act 2008 got the President assent on 5 Feb 2009 and was made effective from 27 October 2009.

Objectives of Information Technology Act, 2000

The Information Technology Act 2000 has been enacted with the following objectives:

- To give legal recognition to any transaction this is done by electronic way or use of internet.
- To give legal recognition to digital signature for accepting any agreement via computer.
- To provide facility of filling document online relating

to school admission or registration in employment exchange.

- To facilitate that any company can store their data in electronic storage.
- To stop computer crime and protect privacy of internet users.
- To give legal recognition for keeping books of accounts by bankers and other companies in electronic form.
- To make more power to IPO, RBI and Indian Evidence act for restricting electronic crime.

Applicability / Scope of Information Technology Act, 2000

The Act extends to the whole of India and except as otherwise provided, it also applies to any offence or contravention there under committed outside India by any person.

- Information Technology Act, 2000 is not applicable on the attestation for creating trust via electronic way. Physical attestation is a must.
- IT Act, 2000 is not applicable on the attestation for making will of anybody. Physical attestation by two witnesses is must.
- A contract of sale of any immovable property.
- Attestation for giving power of attorney of property is not possible via electronic record.

Structure of Information Technology Act, 2000

The Act totally has 13 chapters and 90 sections. (Sections 91 to 94 deal with the amendments to the four Acts namely Indian Penal Code 1860, The Indian Evidence Act 1872, The Bankers'

Books Evidence Act 1891 and the Reserve Bank of India Act 1934.) The Act has chapters that deal with authentication of electronic records, electronic and digital signatures etc. Elaborate procedures for certifying authorities and electronic signatures have been spelt out. The civil offence of data theft and the process of adjudication and appellate procedures have been described. Then the Act goes on to define and describe some of the well-known cyber crimes and lays down the punishments therefore. Then the concept of due diligence, role of intermediaries and some miscellaneous provisions have been described.

Rules and procedures mentioned in the Act have also been laid down in a phased manner, with the latest one on the definition of private and sensitive personal data and the role of intermediaries, due diligence etc, defined as recently as April 2011.

For the sake of simplicity, here we will be only discussing the various penalty and offences defined as per provisions of ITA 2000 and ITAA 2008. Please note that wherever the terms IT Act 2000 or 2008 are used, they refer to same act because the IT Act now includes amendments as per IT 2008 Amendment Act.

There are 13 chapters in law and all provision is included in this chapters.

Chapter Number	Chapter Details	Explanation
Chapter I	Preliminary	Deals with the introduction applicability and Scope of the Act.
Chapter II	Digital Signature and Electronic Signature	This chapter states that any contract which is done by subscriber can be executed through online medium too; if he signs the electronic agreement by digital signature. Then it will be valid and will be called e-contract. In this case the verification of digital signature can be on the basis of key pair.
Chapter III	Electronic Governance	This chapter explains the detail that all electronic records of government are acceptable unless any other law has any rules regarding written or printed record.

Chapter IV	Attribution, knowledgement and Dispatch of Electronic Records	This chapter deals with receipts or acknowledgement of any electronic record. Every electronic record has any proof that is called receipt and it should be in the hand who records electronic way.
Chapter V	Secure Electronic Records and Secure Electronic Signatures	This chapter discusses the powers to organization for securing the electronic records and secure digital signature. They can secure by applying any new verification system.
Chapter VI	Regulation of Certifying Authorities	This chapter states that Government of India will appoint controller of certifying authorities and he will control all activities of certifying authorities. "Certifying authority is that authority who issues digital signature certificate."

Chapter VII	Electronic Signature Certificates	In this chapter powers and duties of certifying authority is given. Certifying Authority (C.A.) will issue digital signature certification after getting Rs. 25000. If it is against public interest, then C.A. can suspend the digital signature certificate.
Chapter VIII	Duties of Subscribers	This chapter tells about the duties of subscribers regarding digital signature certificate. It is the duty of subscriber to accept that all information in digital signature certificate that is within his knowledge is true.
Chapter IX	Penalties, Compensation and Adjudication	If anybody or group of body damages the computers, computer systems and computer networks by electronic hacking, then they are responsible to pay penalty upto Rs. 1 crore.

Chapter X	The Cyber Appellate Tribunal	Under this chapter, provisions are given to establish cyber regulation appellate tribunal. It will solve the cases relating to orders of adjudicating officers.
Chapter XI	Offences	For controlling Cyber Crime, government can appoint cyber regulation advisory committee who will check all cyber crime relating to publishing others information. If any fault is done by anybody, he will be liable for paying Rs. 2 lakh or punishment of 3 years imprisonment or both.
Chapter XII	Intermediaries not to be liable in certain cases	The Chapter states that in certain cases intermediaries' cannot to be held liable. This chapter owes its genesis from the Bazee.com case.

Chapter XII-A	Examination of Electronic Evidences	Police officers have also power to investigate dangerous cyber crime under Indian Penal Code, 1860; Indian Evidence Act, 1872; and Reserve Bank of India Act, 1934.
Chapter XIII	Miscellaneous	

Common Cyber Crimes scenarios and Applicability of Legal Sections: A Snapshot

Let us look into some common cyber crime scenarios which can attract prosecution as per the penalities and offences prescribed in IT Act 2000 (amended via 2008) Act.

Sr. No.	Cyber Crime	Applicable Provisions
1.	**Harassment via fake public profile on social networking site:** A fake profile of a person is created on a social networking site with the correct address, residential information or contact details but he/she is labelled as 'prostitute' or a person of 'loose character'. This leads to harassment of the victim.	Sections 66A, 67 of IT Act and Section 509 of the Indian Penal Code.
2.	**Online Hate Community:** Online hate community is created inciting a religious group to act or pass objectionable remarks against a country, national figures etc.	Section 66A of IT Act and 153A & 153B of the Indian Penal Code.
3.	**Email Account Hacking:** If victim's email account is hacked and obscene emails are sent to people in victims address book.	Sections 43, 66, 66A, 66C, 67, 67A and 67B of IT Act.

4.	**Credit Card Fraud:** Unsuspecting victims would use infected computers to make online transactions.	Sections 43, 66, 66C, 66D of IT Act and Section 420 of the Indian Penal Code.
5.	**Web Defacement:** The homepage of a website is replaced with a pornographic or defamatory page. Government sites generally face the wrath of hackers on symbolic days.	Sections 43 and 66 of IT Act and Sections 66F, 67 and 70 of IT Act also apply in some cases.
6.	**Introducing Viruses, Worms, Backdoors, Rootkits, Trojans, Bugs:** All of the above are some sort of malicious programs which are used to destroy or gain access to some electronic information.	Sections 43, 66, 66A of IT Act and Section 426 of Indian Penal Code.
7.	**Cyber Terrorism:** Many terrorists use virtual (G-Drive, FTP sites) and physical storage media (USB's, hard drives) for hiding information and records of their illicit business.	Conventional terrorism laws may apply along with Section 69 of IT Act.

8.	**Online sale of illegal articles:** Where sale of narcotics, drugs weapons and wildlife is facilitated by the Internet.	Generally conventional laws apply in these cases.
9.	**Cyber Pornography:** Among the largest businesses on Internet. Pornography may not be illegal in many countries, but child pornography is prohibited at large.	Sections 67, 67A and 67B of the IT Act.
10.	**Phishing and Email Scams:** Phishing involves fraudulently acquiring sensitive information through masquerading a site as a trusted entity. (E.g. Passwords, credit card information)	Section 66, 66A and 66D of IT Act and 420 of Indian Penal Code.
11.	**Theft of Confidential Information:** Many business organizations store their confidential information in computer systems. This information is targeted by rivals, criminals and disgruntled employees.	Sections 43, 66, 66B of IT Act and Section 426 of Indian Penal Code.

12.	**Source Code Theft:** A source code generally is the most coveted and important "Crown Jewel" asset of a company.	Sections 43, 66, 66B of IT Act and Section 63 of Copyright Act.
13.	**Tax Evasion and Money Income Tax Act and Laundering:** Money launderers and people doing illegal business activities hide their information in virtual as well as physical activities.	Prevention of Money Laundering Act IT Act may apply case-wise.
14.	**Online Share Trading Fraud:** It has become mandatory for investors to have their demat accounts linked with their online banking accounts which are generally accessed unauthorized, thereby leading to share trading frauds.	Sections 43, 66, 66C, 66D of IT Act and Section 420 of Indian Penal Code.

Final Note

It is quite clear that increasing tendencies of cyber crime without legal recourse are detrimental to the growth of electronic transactions in our country at par with global standards. Therefore, a balanced law on preventing and regulating cyber crime is need of the hour.

The law on cyber crime needs to be strong in order to prevent future cyber crime. Law should change it recourse to ensure a safe, secure and trustworthy computing environment. It is crucial not only to our national sense of well-being, but also to our national security and economy.

Though India has taken a lot of steps to stop cybercrime but the cyber law cannot afford to be static, it has to change with the changing times.

Best practice to prevent cyber crime should include, but not limited to, following directions:

- Updating the Computer System Regularly;
- Selecting strong passwords which cannot be guessed. One should avoid using passwords like date of birth, date of marriage anniversary and alike;
- Keep changing the passwords regularly; at a minimum of 60 days;
- Protecting Computers with security softwares and physical firewalls;

- Protecting ones personal information;
- Keeping an eye on phony email messages;
- Regular signing out of online accounts and transactions;
- Avoid sharing credit card and debit card details;
- Stop responding to emails and messages asking for personal information;
- Pay attention to privacy policies;
- Guarding ones email addresses;
- Regularly reviewing bank and credit card statements and transaction reports and alike

Promoting #CyberLiteracy

Last but not the least; the government should start campaigns in promoting literacy about cyber world and cyber crime specifically to make the people more aware about the use and misuse. It is further recommended that cyber literacy should start from grassroots level; institutes, computer centers, schools & individuals.

Therefore, along with strengthening the legal protection on cyber crimes, the government should enhance the awareness amongst masses about the use and misuse of Information and Communication Technology and its recompense and effects in the inclusive development of nation as a whole. This will surely commence us towards a true "Digital India."

Appendix A: IT Act 2000

1. **Penalties, Compensation and Adjudication sections**

- **Section 43 – Penalty and Compensation for damage to computer, computer system**
  If any person without permission of the owner or any other person who is in-charge of a computer, computer system or computer network –

    - Accesses or secures access to such computer, computer system or computer network or computer resource

    - Downloads, copies or extracts any data, computer data, computer database or information from such computer, computer system or computer network including information or data held or stored in any removable storage medium;

    - Introduces or causes to be introduced any computer contaminant or computer virus into any computer, computer system or computer network-

    - Damages or causes to be damaged any computer, computer system or computer network, data, computer database, or any other programmes residing in such computer, computer system or computer network-

- Disrupts or causes disruption of any computer, computer system, or computer network;
- Denies or causes the denial of access to any person authorised to access any computer, computer system or computer network by any means
- Charges the services availed of by a person to the account of another person by tampering with or manipulating any computer of a computer, computer system or computer network-
- Provides any assistance to any person to facilitate access to a computer, computer system or computer network in contravention of the provisions of this Act, rules or regulations made there under,
- Charges the services availed of by a person to the account of another person by tampering with or manipulating any computer, computer system, or computer network,
- Destroys, deletes or alters any information residing in a computer resource or diminishes its value or utility or affects it injuriously by any means,
- Steals, conceals, destroys or alters or causes any person to steal, conceal, destroy or alter any computer source code used for a computer resource with an intention to cause damage,

he shall be liable to pay damages by way of compensation to the person so affected.

- **Section 43A – Compensation for failure to protect data** Where a body corporate, possessing, dealing or handling any sensitive personal data or information in a computer resource which it owns, controls or operates, is negligent in implementing and maintaining reasonable security practices and procedures and thereby causes wrongful loss or wrongful gain to any person, such body corporate shall be liable to pay damages by way of compensation, not exceeding five crore rupees, to the person so affected.

- **Section 44 – Penalty for failure to furnish information or return, etc.** If any person who is required under this Act or any rules or regulations made there under to –

    - Furnish any document, return or report to the Controller or the Certifying Authority, fails to furnish the same, he shall be liable to a penalty not exceeding one lakh and fifty thousand rupees for each such failure;

    - File any return or furnish any information, books or other documents within the time specified therefore in the regulations, fails to file return or furnish the same within the time specified therefore in the regulations, he shall be liable to a penalty not exceeding five thousand rupees for every day during which such failure continues:

- Maintain books of account or records, fails to maintain the same, he shall be liable to a penalty not exceeding ten thousand rupees for every day during which the failure continues.

- **Section 45 – Residuary Penalty** Whoever contravenes any rules or regulations made under this Act, for the contravention of which no penalty has been separately provided,shall be liable to pay a compensation not exceeding twenty-five thousand rupees to the person affected by such contravention or a penalty not exceeding twenty-five thousand rupees.

- **Section 47 – Factors to be taken into account by the adjudicating officer** Section 47 lays down that while adjudging the quantum of compensation under this Act, an adjudicating officer shall have due regard to the following factors, namely :-

  - The amount of gain of unfair advantage, wherever quantifiable, made as a result of the default;

  - The amount of loss caused to the person as a result of the default,

  - The repetitive nature of the default.

Offences sections

- **Section 65 – Tampering with Computer Source Documents** If any person knowingly or intentionally conceals, destroys code or alters or causes another to conceal, destroy code or alter any computer, computer program, computer system, or computer network,he shall be punishable with imprisonment up to three years, or with fine up to two lakh rupees, or with both.

- **Section – 66 Computer Related Offences** If any person, dishonestly, or fraudulently, does any act referred to in section 43,he shall be punishable with imprisonment for a term which may extend to two three years or with fine which may extend to five lakh rupees or with both.
- **Section 66A – Punishment for sending offensive messages through communication service** Any person who sends, by means of a computer resource or a communication device,
    - Any information that is grossly offensive or has menacing character;
    - Any information which he knows to be false, but for the purpose of causing annoyance, inconvenience, danger, obstruction, insult, injury, criminal intimidation, enmity, hatred, or ill will, persistently makes by making use of such computer resource or a communication device,
    - Any electronic mail or electronic mail message for the purpose of causing annoyance or inconvenience or to deceive or to mislead the addressee or recipient about the origin of such messages shall be punishable with imprisonment for a term which may extend to three years and with fine.

- **Section 66B – Punishment for dishonestly receiving stolen computer resource or communication device.** Whoever dishonestly receives or retains any stolen computer resource or communication device knowing or having reason to believe the same to be stolen computer resource or communication device, shall be punished with imprisonment of either description for a term which may extend to three years or with fine which may extend to rupees one lakh or with both.

- **Section 66C: Punishment for identity theft** Whoever, fraudulently or dishonestly make use of the electronic signature, password or any other unique identification feature of any other person, shall be punished with imprisonment of either description for a term which may extend to three years and shall also be liable to fine which may extend to rupees one lakh.

- **Section 66D: Punishment for cheating by personation by using computer resource** Whoever, by means of any communication device or computer resource cheats by personating; shall be punished with imprisonment of either description for a term which may extend to three years and shall also be liable to fine which may extend to one lakh rupees.

- **Section 66E – Punishment for violation of privacy** Whoever, intentionally or knowingly captures, publishes or transmits the image of a private area of any person without his or her consent, under circumstances violating the privacy of that person,Explanation – For the purposes of this section:

a. "transmit" means to electronically send a visual image with the intent that it be viewed by a person or persons;

b. "capture", with respect to an image, means to videotape, photograph, film or record by any means;

c. "private area" means the naked or undergarment clad genitals, pubic area, buttocks or female breast;

d. "publishes" means reproduction in the printed or electronic form and making it available for public;

e. "under circumstances violating privacy" means circumstances in which a person can have a reasonable expectation that–

    i. he or she could disrobe in privacy, without being concerned that an image of his private area was being captured; or

    ii. any part of his or her private area would not be visible to the public, regardless of whether that person is in a public or private place.

shall be punished with imprisonment which may extend to three years or with fine not exceeding two lakh rupees, or with both.

- **Section-66F Cyber Terrorism**

1. Whoever,-

    a. with intent to threaten the unity, integrity, security or sovereignty of India or to strike terror in the people or any section of the people by –

i. denying or cause the denial of access to any person authorized to access computer resource; or

ii. attempting to penetrate or access a computer resource without authorization or exceeding authorized access; o

iii. introducing or causing to introduce any Computer Contaminant and by means of such conduct causes or is likely to cause death or injuries to persons or damage to or destruction of property or disrupts or knowing that it is likely to cause damage or disruption of supplies or services essential to the life of the community or adversely affect the critical information infrastructure specified under section 70, or

b. knowingly or intentionally penetrates or accesses a computer resource without authorisation or exceeding authorized access, and by means of such conduct obtains access to information, data or computer database that is restricted for reasons of the security of the State or foreign relations; or any restricted information, data or computer database, with reasons to believe that such information, data or computer database so obtained may be used to cause or likely to cause injury to the interests of the sovereignty and integrity of India, the security of the State, friendly relations with foreign States, public order, decency or morality, or in relation to contempt of court, defamation or incitement to an offence, or to the advantage of any foreign nation, group of individuals or otherwise, commits the offence of cyber terrorism.

2. Whoever commits or conspires to commit cyber terrorism shall be punishable with imprisonment which may extend to imprisonment for life.

- **Section 67 – Punishment for publishing or transmitting obscene material in electronic form** Whoever publishes or transmits or causes to be published in the electronic form, any material which is lascivious or appeals to the prurient interest or if its effect is such as to tend to deprave and corrupt persons who are likely, having regard to all relevant circumstances, to read, see or hear the matter contained or embodied in it,shall be punished on first conviction with imprisonment of either description for a term which may extend to two three years and with fine which may extend to five lakh rupees and in the event of a second or subsequent conviction with imprisonment of either description for a term which may extend to five years and also with fine which may extend to ten lakh rupees.

- **Section 67A – Punishment for publishing or transmitting of material containing sexually explicit act, etc. in electronic form** Whoever publishes or transmits or causes to be published or transmitted in the electronic form any material which contains sexually explicit act or conduct shall be punished on first conviction with imprisonment of either description for a term which may extend to five years and with fine which may extend to ten lakh rupees and in the event of second or subsequent conviction with imprisonment of either description for a term which may extend to seven years and also with fine which may extend to ten lakh rupees.

- **Section 67B. Punishment for publishing or transmitting of material depicting children in sexually explicit act, etc. in electronic form** Whoever:
    - publishes or transmits or causes to be published or transmitted material in any electronic form which depicts children engaged in sexually explicit act or conduct or
    - creates text or digital images, collects, seeks, browses, downloads, advertises, promotes, exchanges or distributes material in any electronic form depicting children in obscene or indecent or sexually explicit manner or
    - cultivates, entices or induces children to online relationship with one or more children for and on sexually explicit act or in a manner that may offend a reasonable adult on the computer resource or
    - facilitates abusing children online or records in any electronic form own abuse or that of others pertaining to sexually explicit act with children, shall be punished on first conviction with imprisonment of either description for a term which may extend to five years and with a fine which may extend to ten lakh rupees and in the event of second or subsequent conviction with imprisonment of either description for a term which may extend to seven years and also with fine which may extend to ten lakh rupees:

- o Provided that the provisions of section 67, section 67A and this section does not extend to any book, pamphlet, paper, writing, drawing, painting, representation or figure in electronic form

i. The publication of which is proved to be justified as being for the public good on the ground that such book, pamphlet, paper writing, drawing, painting, representation or figure is in the interest of science, literature, art or learning or other objects of general concern; or

ii. which is kept or used for bonafide heritage or religious purposes

- **Section 69 – Powers to issue directions for interception or monitoring or decryption of any information through any computer resource:**

0. Where the Central Government or a State Government or any of its officer specially authorized by the Central Government or the State Government, as the case may be, in this behalf may, if is satisfied that it is necessary or expedient to do in the interest of the sovereignty or integrity of India, defence of India, security of the State, friendly relations with foreign States or public order or for preventing incitement to the commission of any cognizable offence relating to above or for investigation of any offence, it may, subject to the provisions of sub-section (2), for reasons to be recorded in writing, by order, direct any agency of the appropriate Government to intercept, monitor or decrypt or cause to be intercepted or monitored or decrypted any information transmitted received or stored through any computer resource.

1. The procedure and safeguards subject to which such interception or monitoring or decryption may be carried out, shall be such as may be prescribed.

2. The subscriber or intermediary or any person in charge of the computer resource shall, when called upon by any agency which has been directed under sub section (1), extend all facilities and technical assistance to –

   - provide access to or secure access to the computer resource generating, transmitting, receiving or storing such information; or

   - intercept or monitor or decrypt the information, as the case may be; or

   - provide information stored in computer resource.

3. The subscriber or intermediary or any person who fails to assist the agency referred to in sub-section (2) shall be punished with an imprisonment for a term which may extend to seven years and shall also be liable to fine.

- **Section 69A – Power to issue directions for blocking for public access of any information through any computer resource**

0. Where the Central Government or any of its officer specially authorized by it in this behalf is satisfied that it is necessary or expedient so to do in the interest of sovereignty and integrity of India, defense of India, security of the State, friendly relations with foreign states or public order or for preventing incitement to

the commission of any cognizable offence relating to above, it may subject to the provisions of sub-sections (2) for reasons to be recorded in writing, by order direct any agency of the Government or intermediary to block access by the public or cause to be blocked for access by public any information generated, transmitted, received, stored or hosted in any computer resource.

1. The procedure and safeguards subject to which such blocking for access by the public may be carried out shall be such as may be prescribed.
2. The intermediary who fails to comply with the direction issued under sub-section (1) shall be punished with an imprisonment for a term which may extend to seven years and also be liable to fine.

- **Section 69B. Power to authorize to monitor and collect traffic data or information through any computer resource for Cyber Security**

0. The Central Government may, to enhance Cyber Security and for identification, analysis and prevention of any intrusion or spread of computer contaminant in the country, by notification in the official Gazette, authorize any agency of the Government to monitor and collect traffic data or information generated, transmitted, received or stored in any computer resource.
1. The Intermediary or any person in-charge of the computer resource shall when called upon by the agency which has been authorized under sub-section (0), provide technical assistance and extend all facilities

to such agency to enable online access or to secure and provide online access to the computer resource generating, transmitting, receiving or storing such traffic data or information.

2. The procedure and safeguards for monitoring and collecting traffic data or information, shall be such as may be prescribed.

3. Any intermediary who intentionally or knowingly contravenes the provisions of subsection (2) shall be punished with an imprisonment for a term which may extend to three years and shall also be liable to fine.

- **Section 71 – Penalty for misrepresentation** Whoever makes any misrepresentation to, or suppresses any material fact from, the Controller or the Certifying Authority for obtaining any license or Electronic Signature Certificate, as the case may be,shall be punished with imprisonment for a term which may extend to two years, or with fine which may extend to one lakh rupees, or with both.

- **Section 72 – Breach of confidentiality and privacy** Any person who, in pursuant of any of the powers conferred under this Act, rules or regulations made there under, has secured access to any electronic record, book, register, correspondence, information, document or other material without the consent of the person concerned discloses such electronic record, book, register, correspondence, information, document or other material to any other person shall be punished with imprisonment for a term which may extend to two years, or with fine which may extend to one lakh rupees, or with both.

- **Section 72A – Punishment for Disclosure of information in breach of lawful contract** Any person including an intermediary who, while providing services under the terms of lawful contract, has secured access to any material containing personal information about another person, with the intent to cause or knowing that he is likely to cause wrongful loss or wrongful gain discloses, without the consent of the person concerned, or in breach of a lawful contract, such material to any other person shall be punished with imprisonment for a term which may extend to three years, or with a fine which may extend to five lakh rupees, or with both.

- **73. Penalty for publishing electronic Signature Certificate false in certain particulars.**

0. No person shall publish a Electronic Signature Certificate or otherwise make it available to any other person with the knowledge that

    a. the Certifying Authority listed in the certificate has not issued it; or

    b. the subscriber listed in the certificate has not accepted it; or

    c. the certificate has been revoked or suspended, unless such publication is for the purpose of verifying a digital signature created prior to such suspension or revocation

1. Any person who contravenes the provisions of sub-section (0) shall be punished with imprisonment

for a term which may extend to two years, or with fine which may extend to one lakh rupees, or with both.

- **Section 74 – Publication for fraudulen purpose**: Whoever knowingly creates, publishes or otherwise makes available a Electronic Signature Certificate for any fraudulent or unlawful purpose shall be punished with imprisonment for a term which may extend to two years, or with fine which may extend to one lakh rupees, or with both.

- **Section 75 – Act to apply for offence or contraventions committed outside India**

  0. Subject to the provisions of sub-section (1), the provisions of this Act shall apply also to any offence or contravention committed outside India by any person irrespective of his nationality.

  1. For the purposes of sub-section (0), this Act shall apply to an offence or contravention committed outside India by any person if the act or conduct constituting the offence or contravention involves a computer, computer system or computer network located in India.

- **Section 77A – Compounding of Offences.**

  0. A Court of competent jurisdiction may compound offences other than offences for which the punishment for life or imprisonment for a term exceeding three years has been provided under this Act. Provided further that the Court shall not compound any offence where such offence affects the socio-economic conditions of the

country or has been committed against a child below the age of 18 years or a woman.

1. The person accused of an offence under this act may file an application for compounding in the court in which offence is pending for trial and the provisions of section 265 B and 265C of Code of Criminal Procedures, 1973 shall apply.

- **Section 77B – Offences with three years imprisonment to be cognizable**
  Notwithstanding anything contained in Criminal Procedure Code 1973, the offence punishable with imprisonment of three years and above shall be cognizable and the offence punishable with imprisonment of three years shall be bailable.

- **Section 78 – Power to investigate offences**
  Notwithstanding anything contained in the Code of Criminal Procedure, 1973, a police officer not below the rank of Inspector shall investigate any offence under this Act.

Appendix B: Criminal Liability: IT Act 2000

Criminal Liability for misuse of information technology under IT Act, 2000 are as follows:

Section	Offence Name	Description	Penalty
65	Tampering with computer source document	Intentional concealment, destruction or alteration of the computer source code which is required to be kept or maintained by law	Imprisonment up to 3 years or with fine up to 2 lakh Rupees or with both.
66	Hacking with Computer System	Destruction, deletion or alteration of any information residing in a computer resource, decreasing its value or utility or affecting it injuriously by whatever means intentionally or knowingly	Imprisonment up to 3 years or with fine up to 2 lakh Rupees or with both.
67	Publishingof information which is obscene in electronic form	Publication or transmission by a person or through someone else in the electronic form, any material which is lascivious or appeals to the prurient interest or if its effect is such which tends to deprave and	On first conviction with imprisonment up to 5 years and with fine up to 1 lakh Rupees and in the event of a second or

		corrupt persons who are likely, having regard to all relevant circumstances, to read, see or hear the matter contained or embodied in it.	subsequent conviction with imprisonment up to 10 years and also with fine up to 2 lakh Rupees.
71	Misrepresentation to the Controller or the Certifying Authority	Making any misrepresentation to, or suppression of any material fact from, the Controller or the Certifying Authority for obtaining any license or Digital Signature Certificate, as the case may be.	Imprisonment for a term which may extend to 2 years, or with fine up to 1 lakh Rupees, or with both
72	Penalty for breach of confidentiality and privacy	Any person, who, in pursuance of any of the powers conferred under IT Act, has secured access to any electronic record, book, register, correspondence, information or document without the consent of the person concerned discloses such electronic record, book, register, correspondence, information, document to any other person.	Imprisonment for a term which may extend to 2 years, or with fine up to 1 lakh Rupees, or with both

73	Publishing Digital Signature Certificate false in certain particulars	Publishing a Digital Signature Certificate or otherwise making it available to any other person with the knowledge that the Certifying Authority listed in the certificate has not issued it or the subscriber listed in the certificate has not accepted it or the certificate has been revoked or suspended, unless such publication is for the purpose of verifying a digital signature created prior to such suspension or revocation	Imprisonment for a term which may extend to 2 years, or with fine up to 1 lakh Rupees, or with both
74	Publication for fraudulent purpose	Creation, publication or otherwise making available a Digital Signature Certificate for any fraudulent or unlawful purpose.	Imprisonment for a term which may extend to 2 years, or with fine up to 1 lakh Rupees, or with both.

Appendix C: IPC and Cyber Crimes

Misuse of Information Technology under Indian Penal Code, 1860

Section	Offence Name	Description	Penalty
Various sections		The IT Act amends the IPC. The word document now includes an electronic record. The result is that anyone using forged electronic record or certificates is punishable under the IPC for offences related to false evidences and certificates	Imprisonments for terms which may extend to 10 years or with fine or with both.
120 A	Criminal Conspiracy	Two or more persons agree to do an illegal act or an act by illegal means themselves or through some other persons or means.	Depending on the object of Conspiracy imprisonment for term from 6 months to life imprisonment with or without fine

153 A (1)	Promoting enmity between different groups	By words spoken or written, signs, visible representations or otherwise attempting to promote or promotion of enmity between different groups on grounds of religion, race, domicile, residence, language etc.	Imprisonment for a term which may extend to 3 years, or with fine or with both.
292	Sale, etc., of obscene books, etc.	Selling, hiring, distribution, public exhibition or putting into circulation of obscene material, taking part or receiving profits of such business, advertisement etc.	On first conviction imprisonment up to 2 years with fine of 2000 Rupees on second or sequent conviction imprisonment up to 5 years with fine of 5000 Rupees
295 A	Deliberate and malicious acts, intended to outrage religious feelings of any class	Using words, signs or visible representations with deliberate and malicious intention to outrage religious feelings of a religious class.	Imprisonment for a term which may extend to 3 years, or with fine or with both.

463	Forgery	Making any false electronic record or a part of it with the intention to cause damage or injury to public or any person to commit any fraud or enter into any express or implied contract	Imprisonment for a term which may extend to 2 years, or with fine or with both.
416	Cheating by personation	Cheating by pretending to be some other person or by knowingly substituting one person for another person representing that he or any other person is a person other he or such other person really is. Person personated could be a real or imaginary person.	Imprisonment for a term which may extend to 2 years, or with fine or with both
499	Defamation	Whoever by words either spoken or intended to be read or by signs or by visible representations makes or publishes any imputation concerning any person intending to harm the reputation of such person is said to defame.	Imprisonment for a term which may extend to 2 years, or with fine or with both.

501	Printing or engraving matter known to be defamatory	Printing or engraving any matter knowing or having good reason to believe that such matter is defamatory.	Imprisonment for a term which may extend to 2 years, or with fine or with both.
503	Criminal Intimidation	Threatening another with any injury to his person, reputation or property or to some person in whom one is interested with the intention to cause alarm to that person or causing him to do any illegal act in order to avoid the threat.	Imprisonments for a term which may extend from 2 years till 7 years, with fine or with both depending on the kind of threat given.
505(1), (2)	Statements conducing to public mischief	Making, publishing or circulating any rumour or false report about armed forces of India or with intention to create enmity, hatred or ill-will between classes.	Imprisonment for a term which may extend to 3 years, or with fine or with both.

507	Criminal Intimidation by anonymous comm-unication	Criminal Intimidation by anonymous communication or having taken precaution to conceal name and whereabouts of the person giving threat.	Imprisonments for a term which may extend from 2 years till 7 years, with fine or with both depending on the kind of threat given and 2 years additional imprisonment.
509	Word, gesture or act intended to insult the modesty of a woman	Utterance of words, making of sound, gesture or exhibition of object in order to intrude the privacy or insult the modesty of a woman.	Imprisonment for a term which may extend to 1 year, or with fine or with both.

Appendix D: Cyber Security Policy

Cybers Space is:

- Complex environment of integration between people, software and services.
- Common pool used by citizens, business, critical information infrastructure, military and groups.
- Vulnerable to a wide range of incidents, whether intentional or accidental, manmade or natural, and the information can be exploited by both nation states and non state actors.

Cyber Security Policy:

- Caters to the whole spectrum of ICT users and providers and is an evolving process.
- It serves as an umberalla framework for defining and guiding the actions related to security of cyber space.
- It also enables the individual sectors and organization in designing appropriate cyber security policies to suit their needs.

Policy Makers

Security policy development is a joint or collective operation of all entity of an organization that is affected by its rules. In general, security policies should not be developed by IT team itself as it is responsibility of everyone that has a stake in the security policy should be involved in its development so that they could too, design and frame the policy according to their requirement. During policy creating following entity typically involves:

- **Board:** Company board members must render their advice to some form of a review of policies in response to exceptional or abnormal running condition of business.
- **IT Team:** IT Team members usually are the biggest consumers of the policy information in any company, as it involves making standard around the usage of the computer system, especially security controls.
- **Legal Team:** This team ensure the legal points in the document and guide a particular point of appropriateness in the company.
- **HR Team:** HR team typically obtain a certified term and condition from each employee that they have read and understood the stipulated policy, as the HR team deals with reward and punishment related issues of employees to implement discipline.

Policy Audience

Security policy applies to all senior management, employees, stockholders, consultants and service providers who use company assets. The security policy must be readable, concise and illustrated to be effectively comprehensible to its audience and all employees so that everyone adheres to policies and fulfils their defined role.

Policy Classification

Security policy must be informative, regulative, and advisory in a broad manner.

Policy Audit

Security policy audits assist the company to understand better the threat the organization is exposed to and the effectiveness of your current protection. Security auditing is a high-level analysis of the current project progess and company posture. Auditing is periodically performed to compare existing practices against a security policy to substantiate or verify the effectiveness of security measures. Finally, the goal of a security audit is to provide the company with a verification of best practices already in place.

Policy Enforcement

Enforcement of security policies ensures compliance with the principle and practices dictated by the company because policy, procedure do not work if they are violated.

Policy Awareness

Company employees are often perceived as "soft" target to be compromised, as the human elements the least predictable and easiest to exploit. Trusted employees either "disgruntle" or are framed to provide valuable information of a company. Therefore, one of the most robust storage to combat this exposure of information by employees is "education." When employees duly able to understand that what they should give or what shouldn't give out confidential information, and also know the reason why then the company internal are less likely to be vulnerable. A good security awareness program must be periodically performed and should include all the existing security policies that are mandated to be compliance from employees' end. Moreover, awareness programs should also integrate communication and reminders to employees about what they should and shouldn't reveal to outsiders. In final words, security policy awareness training and education mitigate the threat of information leakage.

Appendix E: Reporting a Cyber Crime

Documents required to make a complaint:

Formal complaint

- Address the complaint to Head of the Cybercrime Cell
- Below details with the application
    - Name
    - Address
    - E-mail address
    - Telephone Number / Mobile Number

Mode of filing complaint

- A complaint can be filed by sending a letter, or online, via email or making a phone call or even an SMS can be sent to the official's number.
- It is advisable that the victim should meet the officials personally as not many cyber complaints are converted into FIRs.

In E-mail related complaints

- A written compliant explaining the complete incidence
- Copy of the alleged e-mail
- E-mail should be taken from the original receiver. Copy of the forwarded e-mail should be avoided
- Full Header of the alleged e-mail

- Copy of e-mail and header should be both hard and soft forms
    - How to view headers
        - In G-Mail
            - Open the e-mail in concern
            - Click the down arrow next to Reply, at the top of the message pane
            - Select Show Original
            - A summry of the headers will appear in a new window
        - In Hotmail
            - Login into your account
            - Select Inbox from the left-side menu
            - Right-click the message you'd like to view headers for and select View Message source
            - The full headers will appear in a new window
        - In Yahoomail
            - Login into your account
            - Select Inbox from the left-side menu
            - Right-click the message you'd like to view headers for and select "View raw message"
            - The full headers will appear in a new window
        - In Rediffmail

            - Login into your account
            - Select Inbox from the left-side menu
            - Open the message you want to see the header and select view header
            - The full headers will appear in a new window

        - In Outlook
            - Login into your account
            - Select Inbox from the left-side menu
            - Open the message you want to see the header and click file tab
            - The full headers will appear in a new window

- Soft copy should be given in a CD-R only

In Social Media related complaints

- Copy / Screenshot of alledged contents / profile
- Screenshot copy of URL of alleged contents
    - How to view URL
        - Click on the image / video / post whose URL you want to view
        - The complete URL will be seen on the address bar
        - Copy the complete URL into a file or document

- Contents should be in both hard and soft forms
- Soft copy should be given in CD-R only

In Mobile Apps related complaints

- Screenshot of the malicious app and the location from where it is downloaded
- Bank Statement from the victim's account if any transactios are made
- Soft copy of all above mentioned documents in soft form

In Business E-mail Compromise complaints

- Brief description of the incident, and consider providing the following financial information:
    - Originating Name
    - Originating Location
    - Originating Bank Name
    - Originating Bank Account Number
    - Recipient Name
    - Recipient Bank Name
    - Recipient Bank Account Number
    - Recipient Bank Location (if available)
    - Intermediary Bank Name (if available)
    - SWIFT Number
    - Date
    - Amount of Transaction
    - Additonal information, if any

In Data Theft complaints

- Copy of data which has been stolen
- Copyright certificate for the data in question
- Details of suspected employee who took the data from company
- Following documents related to suspected employee:

  - Appointment letter
  - Non-Disclosure Agreement (NDA)
  - List of duty assigned
  - List of gadgets assigned to the suspected
  - List of clients with whom the suspect is in touch

- Proof of selling of your copyright data to any client
- Devices used by the suspect while working with the company, if any

In Ransomware complaints

- E-Mail ID / phone number or any other means of communication through which ransom has been demanded
- If malware was sent in the attachment of the mail. Screenshots of the mail with full header of first receiver should be provided

In Net banking / ATM complaints

- Bank statement from the concerned bank of last six months
- Copy of SMSs received related to the alleged transactions
- Copy of your ID proof and address proof as shown in the bank records

In Fake Call Frauds

- Bank statement from the concerned bank of last six months
- Make a copy of SMSs received related to the alleged transactions
- Copy of your ID proof and address proof as shown in the bank records.

In Lottery Scams complaints

- Bank statement from the concerned bank of last six months

- Make a copy of SMSs received related to the alleged transactions
- Copy of your ID proof and address proof as shown in the bank records.

In BitCoin related complaints

- Complete facts in brief about the incident
- Address of Bitcoin
- Amount of Bitcoin involved
- Address from / to whom purchase / sale of Bitcoins is done

In Cheating related complaints

- Printout of the alleged e-mail along with its full header of the e-mail
- E-mail should be taken from the original receiver. Copy of the forwarded e-mail should be avoided
- Bank statement from the victim's account
- Details of the alleged transaction made
- Soft copy of all above mentioned documents

In Online Transactions related complaints

- Bank statement from the concerned bank of last six months
- Make a copy of SMSs received related to the alleged transactions
- Copy of your ID proof and address proof as shown in the bank records

In Hacking compliants

- Website Defaced
    - Copy of the defaced web page in hard and soft form

- Data Compromised on server or computer or any other network equipment
    - Soft copy of the original data
    - Soft copy of compromised data
- Access control mechanism details i.e. who had what kind of the access to the compromised system
- List of suspects – if the victim is having any suspicion on anyone

In Duped by a Company Online related compliants

- Details of the product purchased
- Date and amount of purchase
- Website Name, Company Name and the Contact Details of the company
- Details of how you were duped (if you were offered any job then details of such job)
- Details of other people complaining about the same can also be attached
- Any other important information

From the desk of Arista

Safety Tips – How to avoid Viruses, Trojans, Worms and Spyware

- **Use antivirus or endpoint security software**

  Install antivirus or endpoint security software on all your desktops and servers, and make sure to keep them up to date. New malware can spread extremely quickly, so have an infrastructure in place that can update all the computers in your organization seamlessly, frequently and on short notice.

  To protect against e-mail borne viruses, spam and spyware, run email filtering software at your gateway.

  And don't forget to protect laptop computers, desktop computers and mobile devices used by employees who telecommute.

- **Block file types that often carry malware**

  Block executable file types from being received by email or downloaded from the Internet. It is unlikely that your organization will ever need to receive these types of files from the outside world.

- **Subscribe to an email alert service**

  Consider adding a live malware information feed to your website or intranet so your users know about the very latest computer threats.

- **Use a firewall on all computers**

  Use a firewall to protect computers that are connected to a network. Many worms can enter even a closed network via USB drives, CDs and mobile devices. Laptops and telecommuters will also need firwall protection.

- **Stay up to date with software patches**

  We encourage using automatic (patch) updating, especially in the case of Windows computers. Patches often close loopholes that can make you vulnerable to malware threats.

- **Back up your data regularly**

  Make regular backups of important work and data, and check that the backups were successful. You should also find a safe place to store your backups, preferably off-site in case of fire. If your computer is infected with malware, you will be able to restore any lost programs and data. Any sensitive backups information should be encrypted and physically secured.

- **Implement device control**

  Prevent unauthorized devices from connecting to your computers. Unauthorized devices such as USB drives, music players and mobile phones can carry malware that will infect a computer when plugged in.

Safety Tips – How to avoid Hoaxes

- **Have a policy on virus warnings**

  Set up a policy on virus warnings. For example: "Do not forward any virus warnings of any kind to anyone other than the person responsible for antivirus issues. It doesn't matter if the virus warnings come from an antivirus vendor or have been confirmed by a large computer company or your best friend. A virus warning that comes from any other source should be ignored."

- **Don't forward chain letters**

  Don't forward a chain letter, even if it offers you rewards for doing so or claims to distribute useful information.

Safety Tips – How to secure your data

- **Encrypt your computers, emails and other devices**

  By encrypting your data, you can make sure that only authorized users with the appropriate encryption key or password can access the information. With encryption you can keep your data secure at all times, even if it is stored on a laptop, CD or other device that is lost or stolen, or if it's contained in an intercepted email.

- **Use device and application control**

  Prevent users from accessing peer-to-peer file sharing and USB drives. These are common paths for data loss.

  Only allow computers that comply with your security policy to access your network. This could include requirements for encryption, or device or application control technologies.

- **Block employee access to cloud-based mail services**

  Put controls in place to monitor or block employee use of cloud storage services such as DropBox. These controls should include applying web-based URL filtering, application controls and data encryption. You can prohibit access and transfer of confidential information to largely unsecured cloud-based storage services.

- **Implement outbound content controls**

  Identify the sensitive data you want to control (e.g. any files containing the term "confidential" or credit card numbers) and then decide how these files can be used. For example, you may wish to present the user with a warning about potential data loss, or prevent distribution of the data by email, blogs or forums.

An encryption solution allows users to choose their preferred cloud storage services because the files are always encrypted and the keys are always your own. And because encryption takes place on the client before any data is synchronized, you have full control of the safety of your data.

- **User wireless encryption**

  Configure your office wireless networks to use strong encryption, such as that offered by WPA2. Encourage your employees to do the same on their wireless networks.

Safety Tips – How to avoid spam

- **Use email filtering software at your email gateway**

  You should run email filtering software at the email gateway to protect your organization from spam as well as email borne spyware, viruses and worms.

- **Never make a purchase from an unsolicited email**

  By making a purchase, you are funding future spam. Spammers may add your e-mail address to lists to sell to other spammers, so that you receive even more junk e-mail. Worse still, you could be the victim of the fraud.

- **If you do not know the sender of an unsolicitied e-mail, delete it**

  Spam can contain malware that damages or compromises the computer when the e-mail is opened.

- **Don't use the preview mode in your e-mail viewer**

  Many spammers can track when a message is viewed, even if you don't click on the e-mail. The preview setting effectively opens the e-mail and lets spammers know that you receive their messages. When you check your e-mail, try to devide whether a message is spam on the basis of the subject line only.

- **Don't over expose your e-mail address**

  How much online exposure you give your e-mail address is the biggest factor in how much spam you receive. Here are some bad habits that expose your e-mail address to spammers:

- Posting to mailing lists that are archived online
- Submitting your address to online services with questionable privacy policies
- Exposing your address publicly on social networks (Facebook, LinkedIn, etc.)
- Using an easily guessable address based on first name, last name and company
- Not keeping your work and personal e-mail separate

- **Use the BCC field if you e-mail many people at once**

  The BCC or blind carbon copy field hides the list of recipients from other users. If you put the addresses in the To field, spammers may harvest them and add them to mailing lists.

- **Use one or two secondary e-mail addresses**

  If you fill out web registration forms or surveys on sites from which you don't want further information, use a secondary e-mail address. This protects your mail address from spam.

- **Opt out of further information or offers**

  When you fill out forms on websites, look for the checkbox that lets you choose whether to accept further information or offers. Check or uncheck the box as appropriate.

Safety Tips – How to avoid being phished

- **Never respond to e-mails that request personal financial information**

  You should be suspicious of any e-mail that asks for your password or account information, or includes links for that purpose. Banks and e-commerce companies do not usually send such e-mails.

- **Look for signs that an e-mail is "phishy"**

  Some phishing e-mails are generic, using greetings like "Dear Valued Customer." They may also include alarming claims (e.g. your account numbers have been stolen), use suspiciously poor spelling or grammar and/or request that you take an action like clicking a link or sending personal information to an unknown address.

  Other phishing e-mails are more targeted and may be very believable. Look for unusual behaviour, such as a blank or irrelevant attachment (which could have hidden malware), or a request to click a link that doesn't fit with the topic or sender of the message.

- **Visit bank websites by typing the address into the address bar**

  Don't follow links embedded in an unsolicited e-mail. Phishers often use these to direct you to a bogus site. Instead, you should type the full address into the address bar in your browser.

- **Keep a regular check on your accounts**

Regularly login to your online accounts and check your statements. If you see any suspicious transactions, report them to your bank or credit card provider.

- **Make sure that the website you are visting is secure**

  Check the web address in the address bar. If the website you are visting is on a secure server, it should start with https:// ("S" stands for secure) rather than the usual http://

  Also look for a small padlock icon on the browser's status bar. These signs tell you that the website is using encryption.

  However, even if a site is secured, there is no guarantee that it is safe because hackers can create websites that use encryption that are designed to steal personal information.

- **Be cautious with e-mails and personal data**

  Always conduct transactions safely. Don't let anyone know your PINs or passwords, do not write them down, and do not use the same password for all your online accounts. Don't open or rely to spam e-mails as this lets the sender know that your address is valid and can be used for future scams.

- **Keep your computer safe**

  Anti-spam software will prevent many phishing e-mails from reaching you. A firewall also helps to keep your personal information secure and block unauthorized communications. You should also run antivirus software to detect and disable malicious programs, such as spyware or backdoor Trojans, which may be included in phishing e-mails. Keep your internet browser up-to-date with the latest security patches.

- **Always report suspicious activity**

If you receive an e-mail you suspect isn't genuine, forward it to the spoofed organization. Many computers have a dedicated e-mail address for reporting such abuse.

Safety Tips – How to be safe on the Internet

This section gives general advice on safely using e-mail and the web. You should also see our tips on How to avoid being phished and How to avoid viruses, Trojans, worms and spyware.

- **Keep up-to-date with security patches**

  Hackers frequently exploit vulnerabilities in operating systems and programs in an attempt to infect computers. Be aware of security updates for your computer's operating system, browser, plugins and other code that could be the target of hackers. If you can, set up your computer to automatically download security patches.

- **Use firewalls**

  A network firewall is installed at your organiation's boundary and admits only authorized types of traffic. A client firewall is installed on each computer on your networks, and also allows only authorized traffic, blocking hackers and Internet worms. In addition, it prevents the computer from communicating with the Internet via unauthorized programs.

- **Don't follow links in unexpected e-mails**

  Links in unexpected e-mails can take you to bogus websites, where any confidential information you enter, such as account numbers and passwords, can be stolen and misused.

  In addition, hackers often try to direct you to malicious webpages by spamming out links via e-mail.

- **Use different passwords for every site**

  You should use a different password for each site where you

have a user account. That way, if a password is compromised, only one account will be affected. In addition, make sure that your passwords are hard to guess and never use a dictionary word as your password.

- **Consider blocking access to certain websites or types of web content**

  In a company environment, you may want to prevent users from accessing sites that are inappropriate for workplace use, or that may pose a security threat (e.g. by installing spyware on computers). You can do this with web filtering software or a hardware appliance. Even if users are allowed to visit websites, you should make sure that all webpages they visit are scanned for security threats.

- **Scan e-mail for malware and spam**

  Anti-spam programs can detect unwanted e-mail and prevent it from reaching users' inboxes, as well as scan for malware contained within the email.

- **Don't click on pop-up messages**

  If you see unsolicited pop-ups, such as message warning that a computer is infected and offering virus removal, don't follow links or click to accept software downloads. Doing so could result in you downloading malicious code such as fake anti-virus software.

- **Use Routers**

  You can use a router to limit connections between the Internet and specific computers. Many routers also incorporate a network firewall.

Safety Tips – How to choose secure passwords

Passwords are your protection against fraud and lots of confidential information, but few people choose passwords that are really secure.

- **Make your password as long as possible**

  The longer a password is, the harder it is to guess or to find by trying all possible combination (i.e. a brute force attack). Passwords of at least 8 characters or more are vastly more difficult to crack.

- **Use different tyes of characters**

  Include numbers, punctuation marks, symbols and uppercase and lowercase letters. On mobile devices that are not designed for easy special character input, consider using longer passwords with different characters.

- **Don't use dictionary words**

  Don't use words, names or place names that are usually found in dictionaries. Hackers can use a dictionary attack (i.e. trying all the words in the dictionary automatically) to crack these passwords.

- **Don't use personal information**

  Other people are likely to know information such as your birthday, the name of your partner or child or your phone number and they might guess that you have used them as a password.

- **Don't use your username**

Don't use a password that is the same as your username or account number.

- **Use passwords that are difficult to identify as you type them in**

  Make sure that you don't use repeated characters or keys close together on the keyboard.

- **Consider using a passphrase**

  A passphrase is a string of words, rather than a single word. Unlikely combinations of words can be hard to guess.

- **Try to memorize your password**

  Memorize your password rather than writing it down. Use a string of characters that is meaningful to you, or use mnemonic devices to help you recall the password. There are good free programs available that will help you manage your passwords.

- **Use a different password for each account**

  If a hacker cracks one of your passwords, at least only one account has been compromised.

- **Don't tell anyone else your password**

  If you receive a request to confirm your password, even if it appears to be from a trustworthy institution or someone within your organization, you should never disclose your password.

- **Don't use your password on a public computer**

Don't enter your password on a publicly available computer (e.g. in a hotel or internet café). Such computers may not be secure and may have keystroke loggers installed.

- **Change your passwords regularly**

  The shorter or simpler your password is, the more often you should replace it.

Safety Tips – How to use removable media securely

- **Educate users**

  Many users are not aware of the potential dangers from removable media such as USBs and CDs / DVDs that spread malware and cause data loss. Educating users help reduce the risks significantly.

- **Identify device types**

  Computers interact with a growing variety of removable media including USB drives, MP3 players and smartphones. Having visibility of what removable media is attempting to connect to your network can help you set appropriate restrictions or permissions.

- **Implement device control**

  Controlling the type of removable media that is permitted and what data is allowed to be exchanged is a vital component of network security. Choose solutions that can set permissions (or restrictions) for individual devices as well as entire classes of devices.

- **Encrypt your data**

  Data encryption prevents the loss of data. This is particularly useful for removable media that can be easily misplaced or stolen because the data cannot be viewed or copied by unauthorized third parties.

Safety Tips – How to buy online safely

- **Can you trust your common sense and intuition?**

  Unfortunately, it isn't practical for users to determine if a website is safe or not with the naked eye.

  Although invisible to the visiting online customer, hackers often target improperly secured legitimate websites. Being a large, well-established company is no guarantee that the site is safe.

  Purchasing from a secure computer or device running the latest antivirus software, firewalls and security patches will significantly decrease your chances of becoming a victim.

  Never follow links from unsolicited online communications, such as email messages, social media posts, or instant messages. Spammers and hackers use social engineering techniques as lures to fraudulent or infected websites.

  Only part with sensitive information like your personal or financial details when you are fully satisfied with the legitimacy of the company.

- **Familiarize yourself with the terms of use and the data protection policy**

  Read the fine print. Terms can sometimes detail hidden and unexpected costs or obligations.

- **Only purchase through websites using encryption**

  URLs that start with https:// rather than http:// (the "s" stands for secure) are encrypting information during transfer. Another indicator of a website using encryption is a small padlock icon displayed in the Internet browser.

However, there is no guarantee that these sites are safe, as hackers can create websites that use encryption but are designed to steal personal information.

- **Provide the minimum amount of personal information**

  Leave optional fields blank: Middle name, date of birth, mobile phone number, hobbies. Many website operators request optional information alongside required information to process a business transaction. Compulsory fields are often identifiable by an asterisk.

- **Never share your password**

  Even if someone else is making the purchase for you, you should enter the password yourself and never share it with others.

  To stop subsequent users from accessing your account without authorization, never select the "remember my password" option on a shared computer.

- **Buy local where possible**

  When the seller is based in a different country, it can be much more difficult and expensive to resolve any issues and to enforce consumer rights legislation.

- **Check your bank statements**

  Check your bank account transactions regularly, particularly after making purchases over the Internet, to be sure that all payments are legitimate. If you discover payments that you cannot identify, inform your bank immediately.

- **Keep your oder confirmation and receipts**

  Always retain important information relating to a purchase in either printed or electronic format. This information will be very useful in resolving any issues relating to the purchase.

Safety Tips – How to stay safe on the move

- **Educate Users**

  Don't underestimate the risks of data loss from unsecured laptops or removable media. Organizations should develop clear policies concerning the use of mobile devices.

- **Use secure passwords**

  Passwords are the very first walls of defense and should always be as strong as possible.

- **Implement additional security checks**

  Smartcards or tokens require you to enter additional information (e.g., a token code together with your password) in order to access your computer. With fingerprint readers, you need to confirm your identity using your fingerprint when booting up or logging in.

- **Encrypt all important data**

  If your data is encrypted, it will remain safe even if your laptop or removable media is lost or stolen. If you don't want to encrypt your entire hard drive, you can create a virtual disk to store confidential information securely.

- **Restrict Plug and Play**

  Plug and Play allows USB drives, MP3 players or external hard drives to connect to laptops automatically, making it easy for data to be copied. Instead, lock the computer so only authorized devices are allowed to connect.

- **Secure remote connections**

  It is easy for nosy individuals to eavesdrop on wireless networks in airports, cafes, hotels and other public places. Secure communications with your organization's servers by using a virtual private network (VPN) configured on each laptop or mobile device. Some applications and websites can also be secured through the use of SSL to encrypt communications.

Safety Tips – How to secure mobile workforce

Smartphones are standard business tools storing sensitive business information and enabling email on the move. This makes them vulnerable to attack from malware; authors seeking out new ways to defraud users and steal confidential business data.

While mobile viruses and spyware remain a relatively small problem compared with the much larger amount of malware targeting Windows computers, the risks to business reputation, communication and continuity are becoming more serious. Risks include data theft, disruption of mobile phone networks and the hijacking of phones to send unauthorized revenue-generating SMS messages. Mobile devices can be infected in many ways including email, MMS, external memory cards, PC synchronization and even via Bluetooth.

Make sure your security policy includes a strategy for mobile devices, covering:

- Threat management - identification and removal of viruses, spyware and spam
- Device access control and management - enforcing a password policy and application management
- Data protection - encryption of sensitive data on devices and remote data deletion
- Network access control - controlling VPN connections across public networks, validation of devices when they connect to the corporate network

Safety Tips for Children

- Never share your personal details like house address, phone number, date of birth and place of birth etc. on any online platform such as Facebook, Instagram, Blogs, Twitter etc.
- Make sure that indecent / offending / harassing e-mails / chat posts are not responded. Rather keep them in records in the form of screenshots and inform your parent / guardian to report it to the police. The account should be immediately blocked.
- When you feel uncomfortable with any social media post / mail / chatting, immediately share your concern with your parents or any trustworthy person.
- Never share your account passwords with anyone.
- Be aware that information on the Internet is not always reliable.
- Make a strong password with alpha-numeric symbols and special characters.
- Don't add people as online friends unless you know them in real life or have parent permission.
- Never agree to meet an online friend unless and until you do so under your parent's / guardian's guidance and supervision.
- Treat others online the way you'd like to be treated yourself. Real life etiquettes and manners apply equally to the virtual space.
- Don't sign up for sites that require a certain age criterion for registration e.g. Facebook, YouTube, Instagram etc. by wrong reporting of your correct age, such sites may expose you to age inappropriate content.

- Don't buy anything online without discussion with your parents. Some advertisement may try to trick you by offering things at heavy discount. They may be fraud sites meant for either cheating you of your parents' money or for getting access to your and your parents' personal information.

Safety Tips for Women

- Choose a safe online name. Pick a name that doesn't reflect your complete identity or location.
- Have a strong password with alpha-numeric symbol and special characters for your online account.
- Secure your computers with anti-virus, anti-spyware and other cyber security tools.
- Be selective about what information you make public. Be cautious while posting online any information that can personally identify you, a family member, or friend on a public site like a blog, or online white pages, or job hunt sites, or in any other place. Anyone on the Internet can see the information. Sensitive information includes real name, date of birth, gender, town, e-mail address, school name, place of work, and personal photos. Fraudsters, cheats and online perverts can misuse this information to your detriment.
- Pay attention to the risks associated with e-mails and think twice before you open attachments or click links in e-mail-even if you know the sender-as these can be used to transmit spam and viruses to your computer.
- Never respond to e-mail asking you to provide personal information, especially your account number or password, even if it seems to be from a business you trust. Reputable businesses will not ask you this information in e-mail. Never click on links provided in an email, unless you are sure of the sender and the purpose of email. Instead, use a search engine to find the site. Don't forward spam, whether it's a cute 'thought of the day', 'set of jokes', 'amazing photo', 'recipe tree' or similar email, if you don't personally know the sender. The email may be a scam designed to collect the email accounts – and relationships – of everyone you share it with.

- Never, try to meet a person with whom you've interacted only online without taking somebody else along and such meeting must always be in a public place. Remember, people are not always who they say they are. People often feel uncomfortable setting safety boundaries because they don't want to offend someone; but good intentioned people will understand and encourage you to set safety requirements, and it is the crooks who want you to feel guilty about it.
- Know the Privacy Policy and Terms of Service of any service you use. Create an environment of safety for yourself by understanding how a website that you use, treats your privacy and information. That fine print may tell you the company can own, resell, rent, or give your information to anyone they want. If it does that then find a more respectful site.
- Don't trade personal information for "freebies." Online freebies come in two forms:
    - The free games, free offers, and great deals. Just as in the physical world, if these types of offers sound too good to be true, they probably are. Not only will these collect and sell your personal information, these 'deals', and 'free' applications are usually riddled with spyware, viruses or other malicious software.
    - Through survey's, sweepstakes, quizzes, and the like. These marketing tools are designed for one purpose – to get as much information from you as they can, so they can sell that to interested parties. Even the most innocuous surveys learn far more than you imagine, and they may give you malicious software or download tracking cookies, so just skip these entirely.

- Periodically review your internet contacts and online activities. Internet housekeeping is important. Periodically review who you have as contacts, and who can see your online profiles periodically to prune out everyone you no longer have a close interaction with. Review images and content, you've posted online to see if collectively these tell more about you than what should be known.
- Block people you don't want to interact with. You don't have to accept invitations to be friends with people just because they ask. People can find it difficult to turn someone down – and creeps and crooks count on this very thing. If you don't want to be friends, delete the request. If you are already connected with someone you would rather not be, block them from your social sites. You can also block their email account so that they can never contact you through email, and block their phone number from calling or sending text messages to your phone. YOU get to choose who, how, and when you are contacted.
- Note that if you become a victim of a cybe crime, it is not your fault. If you fall victim to a scam, fraudster, abuser or criminal, don't blame yourself. The only person guilty is the abuser or a criminal. You didn't cheat, scam, lie, threaten, harm, steal, or abuse yourself in some other way, so don't lay a burden of guilt. Don't let the abuser or the criminal shame you into silence. Speak out and get the help you need.
- Don't post personal information such as mobile numbers and personal email ids on social networking sites.
- Be extremely cautious while posting photographs and control who can view them. Bear in mind that photos can be saved and altered – you don't want to regret having posted a particular photo, at a later stage! Create restricted user

groups who can view photos. Also, don't post embarrassing pictures of others.

- Use strong passwords and use different passwords for different accounts. Social networking sites are very easily hacked into and information can be modified. So, ensure that you don't use weak passwords with personal information such as your birthday or your dog's name. Your password should be one that is difficult to guess.
- Don't share your password with anyone or let anybody else handle your account. What is seen as trust or some harmless fun, can have severe consequences.
- Don't accept "friend requests" from people totally unknown to you and from those that you don't want to interact with. If you are being bothered by someone already on your friend's list, feel free to block them! You get to choose who you want to interact with; don't be "nice" and put up with any inconvenience.
- Ensure your computer has a good antivirus and anti spyware software. A lot of applications on social networking sites can be malicious, and if your computer is not well protected, it can result in a lot of issues.
- Remember that information that you post once on the internet cannot be erased. Use your common sense and utmost caution when you publish anything. A lot of cyber crime can be prevented simply by exercising caution.
- If you notice any offensive, abusive or illegal online post/ content, immediately take its screenshot. Also take a screenshot of the link/URL of the illegal content.
- On social media make friends with people whom you personally know. Many times, we accept friend requests from friends of friends. However, even your friends may not be knowing them and had accepted their friend request

because it was a friend of friend. Such unrecognizable friend may be cheats and perverts who may misuse your 'friend' privileges and access on Social Media to harm you in many ways.

- Don't click on links sent over Facebook Messenger or other messages services, even if they are sent from your friend's account, if they are unsolicited (i.e you have neither asked for it nor were you expecting it). Note: even your friend's account may have been hacked and used from hackers to spread malware to unsuspecting 'friend'.
- Don't share any OTP or other passwords, even with 'friend' on any pretext. Such 'pretext' are tricks used by hackers to deceive you through social engineering in sharing your passwords, which may have grave consequences, such as loss of control over social media account, your email account ID, etc.
- On social media accounts keep your privacy settings to the most stringent levels. Only share information about yourself on 'Need to Know' basis.
- On WhatsApp and other messaging Apps, ensure that 'media auto-download' is deactivated, especially, from senders who are not in your contact list. Such media (videos, photos, documents, etc.) may have malwares embedded in them.
- Always keep your device (Phone, Tablet, Laptop etc.) in safe custody. Keep your lock screen on with password/PIN protection. Don't keep your device unattended even for a minute.
- Note: Information posted online can never be completely removed. So, apply caution while sharing anything online.
- Note: The online audience is much larger than we comprehend. Anything offensive or embarrassing, has a higher chance of becoming viral and out of control.

Apply caution while posting things online about other people.

- Last, but not the least, trust your instinct. If you are being subjected to any form of cyber bullying or harassment, report it at once!

Safety Tips for Senior Citizens

- Are you a senior citizen who is active on Social Media? Have you off-late become friends with individuals from other countries (whom you don't know in real life) and these online friends have been really caring and emotionally supportive? Have you ever wondered how these online oversees 'friends' have suddenly come into your life and become your emotional support? Well, many a time, these 'friends' are fraudsters who are spinning on elaborate web of deceit around you. They will, on some pretext or the other, trick you and emotionally blackmail you to share your hard-earned retirement money with them. Don't fall for such elaborate frauds. Apply the real-world caution that you have learned over the years to virtual space too.
- Make sure your computer has security software on it and also check that the auto-update feature is enabled to ensure that your computer has the latest security features.
- Passwords need to be unique and strong – these passwords need to be made up of upper- and lower-case letters as well as numbers. Never reveal your password to anyone. Passwords are an excellent guarantee of safety and security online.
- Post with caution on social networking sites. It is a good idea to also understand how privacy settings work on social networks.
- Don't automatically install a software because it is free – these types of software are generally riddled with spyware which can slow or crash your computer.
- Attachments can contain a virus and the virus can be transmitted to your computer as soon as you open the attachment. Be wary of suspect attachments, even from people you may know. If an email or attachment seems

suspicious, don't open it. Online criminals often use e-mails to get personal information from you in order to steal your identity. Sometimes these emails will invite you to click a link which downloads malware to your computer.

- Although online banking is very convenient for seniors, be sure to only enter information into security-enabled sites. Sites for instance which begin with https:// means that the data is encrypted in transit. Look out for this and don't enter any bank details or credit card information into websites that start only with http://
- Emotional abuse is as rife online as it is elsewhere. It is best not to satisfy the abuser with any kind of response.
- Never trust a link sent to you by someone you don't know. By clicking the link, you may be taken to a site that may look like your bank or credit card company, but it is not. One thing a criminal can't fake is the actual website address of a company or bank. Instead of clicking a link in an e-mail, search for the Web address using a search engine such as google to find the real one. Ask the company about the message you received, or call using the number listed on your statements. Mark the real site as a favorite in your browser so that one click brings you there safely every time.
- Never trust an e-mail that asks for your personal or account information (called a phishing scam). These usually seem convincing (the shabby ones have spelling errors, but the high-quality scams look impeccable). No bank or reputable company is going to send you an e-mail asking you to correct your information, validate your identity, re-enter your password, and so on.
- The smarter scams often contain text, warning you against fraud. They do this because many people believe that an e-mail that warns them to be careful must be legitimate.

That is not always true. This also extends to sites that claim they have protections in place for your privacy and security. Anybody can make these claims, but only certain sites protect you.

- Never respond – or even open an e-mail with a deal that is too good to be true unless it is from a company that you know well and expect to get these kinds of offers from them. Scammers want you to react without taking time to think through, so their e-mails frequently sound urgent, such as:
    - o "if we don't hear by tomorrow your account will be closed" (and you'll notice that the date of "tomorrow" never is listed).
    - o " this offer won't last, order now to ensure"...
- Never believe that someone you don't know is going to give you money.
- Do not believe a person from another country who just needs you to "help transfer funds" and they need your bank account number to do so. Such scammers promise to give you a huge amount of money for helping them out. The result is an empty bank account.
- If you never entered a lottery, you can't win the lottery. Such scams ask you to provide your information and bank account number so they can transfer your prize money. Don't, the result will be an empty bank account.
- Don't believe a really rich, famous person just wants to help you out... and that the celebrity also mysteriously needs your address, phone number, bank account information to do so. The result will be an empty bank account.
- Don't fall prey to fraud calls regarding Insurance Bonus, New policy with better coverage, etc. where the returns/ gains offered are much higher than industry norm. These fraud callers have an eye on your retirement funds and induce you by promising exceptional returns.

Safety Tips for Parents

- Have an open conversation with your kids about safe browsing and computer use.
- Do not replace physical parental supervision of computer use at home with any safe search engine or any other tool. No search filtering software or tool is perfect.
- Educate yourself also on social media safety and have open discussions with teens about present dangers and long-term effects of inappropriate conduct, including posting pictures/videos online.
- Keep computer in an open area. Make a rule that doors are always left open when kids are online.
- Advice your children to immediately exit any site that makes them feel uncomfortable or worried.
- Parent should keep a track of persons with whom their children are talking to and which sites they are browsing. This is NOT invading their privacy at all, rather it is parenting in the digital space.
- If you have found inappropriate content about your child please contact the service provider concerned and/or Police as soon as possible.
- Majority of children would not like to tell their parents if they are bullied or harassed online for fear that they will lose internet access. Make sure that your children understand that they will not get in trouble if they tell you about a problem.
- Children under 13 ARE NOT ALLOWED on Facebook, Instagram, SnapChat, iTunes, YouTube and many more. Don't support your child to break the rules as they are not the only ones without these accounts.
- Explain it to your child that all Social Networking Profiles

MUST BE SET TO PRIVATE. Use all the security settings available to make the site as safe as possible.

- Do not let young children to browse the 'Google' aimlessly with no supervision. Children need to be taught about search engines and how they work.
- Don't allow your child to use Apps like SnapChat that immediately delete the posts. Apps prevent you from monitoring the child's online experience and you may never know what he is being subjected to.
- If you notice a sudden change in your child's behaviour, to check, among other things, his online activity on social media.

Safety Tips for Businesspersons (SME)

- Defend your computers. Keep all softwares (including your Web browser) with automatic updates and install all security updates that your IT department recommends. Use antivirus, antispam, and antispyware software and activate your firewall.
- Think before you share sensitive information. Look for signs that a Web page is safe, before you enter sensitive personal or business data – a Web address with https ("s" for secure) and a closed padlock ( ) beside it. Never give sensitive information in response to an e-mail or instant message (IM) request.
- Think before you click. Pause before you open attachments or click links in e-mail or IM even if you know the sender; they could be phony. Confirm with the sender that the message is real or visit the official Web site by typing the address yourself. Be wary of clicking links or buttons in pop-up windows.
- Use strong passwords. Lock your online accounts, computer, phone, and other devices with passwords of at least eight characters length (longer is better), and include upper- and lower-case letters, numbers, and symbols. Keep passwords and PINs secret. Don't disclose them to coworkers or businesses (like an Internet café operator), or be tricked into giving them away. Don't use the same password everywhere.
- Protect yourself from e-mail scams. Look out for alarmist messages, misspellings and grammatical errors, deals that sound too good to be true, requests for sensitive information like account numbers, and other signs of a scam. Turn on a filter that warns you of suspicious Web sites.

- Protect your data on the go. When you use public Wi-Fi, choose the most secure option, even if you have to pay for it. It could include password-protection and encryption. Confirm the exact spelling of the wireless network you're connecting to. Beware of clever (slightly misspelled) fakes. Encrypt the data on your laptop (or USB flash drive) in case you lose it or it's stolen. Guard your laptop, smartphone, and PDA as carefully as your wallet.
- Restricting the types of websites that employees are allowed to visit can help you exclude the sites that could compromise your network.
- Advise employees about which softwares are safe to be installed on their computer.
- When someone outside of your business requests any personal or business information, verify that he is a safe person with whom information can be sent.
- Write an Internet Usage Policy for personnel to follow and post it in an accessible place for all to see and refer to.
- Set rules on what kinds of business information your employees can share online, and where.
- Create instructions on whether your employees should use their working email to sign up for social media sites and newsletters.
- Consider the implementation of a company social media policy, so that employees know what they should and should not post online.
- Update all of your business softwares when you receive notifications to do so, so that all security fixes are up to date.
- Instruct all of your employees to have complex passwords that have letters, numbers and symbols so they are harder for cyber criminals to steal/crack.

- Always be suspicious of phone calls, emails or other communications from an unknown source.
- Only visit legitimate and trusted websites while using business computers or working with business information.
- Before providing personal information to anyone, verify that they are a trusted source (for example, a bank would not send out personal inquiries by email, so a call to the actual bank might be advised if such an email were received).
- If someone is seeking your personal information, ask why the information is required.
- If the answer does not seem satisfactory, do not provide it — or ask for their supervisor to get more details.
- Never remove or disable any security safeguards put into place on business networks and computers (such as anti-virus software).
- Social networking sites like Facebook, Twitter and LinkedIn can be powerful tools for your business to reach potential customers and build stronger relationships with clients. However, social networking sites and services are becoming an increasingly popular way for cyber criminals to try to get your personal or business information to hack into your personal or business computer systems.
- If your business uses social networking sites for marketing or professional purposes, you will need to choose one or more employees, and only allow them to post content in your business's name.

Safety Tips for Social Media

- Use caution when you click links that you receive in messages from your friends on social website. Treat links in messages on these sites as you would treat links in e-mail messages.
- Always remember what you've posted about yourself. A common way that hackers break into financial or other accounts is by clicking the "Forgot your password?" link on the account login page. To break into your account, they search for the answers to your security questions, such as your birthday, hometown, high school class, father's middle name, on your social networking site. If the site allows, make up your own password questions, and don't draw them from material anyone could find with a quick search.
- Don't trust that a message is really from one who has been shown there. Hackers can break into accounts and send messages that looks like they're from your friends, but they aren't. If you suspect that a message is fraudulent, use an alternate method to contact your friend to find out its veracity. This includes invitations to join new social networks.
- To avoid fetching of e-mail addresses of your friends, do not allow social networking services to scan your e-mail address book. When you join a new social network, you might receive an offer to enter your e-mail address and password to find out if your contacts are on the network. The site might use this information to send e-mail messages to everyone in your contact list or even to everyone you've ever sent an e-mail message with that e-mail address. Social networking sites should explain that they're going to do this, but some do not.
- Type the address of your social networking site directly into

your browser or use your personal bookmarks. If you click a link to your site through e-mail or another website, you might be entering your account name and password into a fake site where your personal information could be stolen.

- Be selective about one whom you accept as a friend on a social network. Identity thieves might create fake profiles in order to get information from you.
- Choose your social network carefully. Evaluate the site that you plan to use and make sure that you understand the privacy policy. Find out if the site monitors content that people post. You will be providing personal information to this website, so carefully examine that the site where you are going to provide details of your credit card.
- Assume that everything you put on a social networking site is permanent. Even if you delete your account, anyone on the Internet can easily print photos or text or save images or screenshots or videos in his device.
- Be careful about installing extras on your site. Many social networking sites allow you to download third-party applications that let you do more with your personal page. Criminals sometimes use these applications to steal your personal information. To download and use third-party applications safely, take the same safety precautions that you take with any other program or file, you download from the Web.
- Think twice before you use social networking sites at work.
- Talk to your kids about social networking & brief them about Do's & Don't's.

Safety Tips for Social Media - Precaution for Businesses (SME)

- Social networking should be addressed in your business's Internet Usage Policy with clear advice to employees. Here are some social networking issues that you should consider:
  - Be clear on what information about your business can be posted and who is authorized to do so.
  - Refrain from including sensitive business information in the business profile or in your posts.
  - Be careful using applications on social networking sites. Many of these come from third parties and may not be secure. Always check on the application provider first.
  - When communicating through social media, be suspicious of any messages that are asking for sensitive business information or about employees and their families.
  - Think before you post! What you post on social media sites is generally permanent. You may someday change your mind about what you said online, but you can't remove or change it permanently as it might have been save as screenshots by someone.
  - Criminals are interested in the information you post. To help your business stay safe, make sure you use the site's privacy controls and ignore requests from people you don't know.
  - Review and stay up to date with the social networking site's privacy policies (most are updated frequently) and adjust personal privacy settings appropriately.
  - Never reveal your precise location online.

Safety Tips for Net Banking Users

- Password protect the mobile phone having your banking application. It is recommended to set the maximum number of incorrect password submissions no more than three.
- Choose a strong password to keep your account and data safe.
- Review your account statements frequently to check for any unauthorized transactions.
- Change your password regularly.
- Report a lost or stolen phone immediately to your service provider and law enforcement authorities.
- Never give your PIN or confidential information over the phone or internet. Never share these details with anyone.
- Don't click on links embedded in emails/social networking sites claiming to be from the bank or representing the bank.
- Don't transfer funds without due validation of the recipient.
- Don't store sensitive information such as credit card details, mobile banking password and user ID in a separate folder on your phone.
- Don't forget to inform the bank of changes in your mobile number to ensure that SMS notifications are not sent to someone else.
- Never reveal or write down PINs or retain any email or paper communication from the bank with regard to the PIN or password.
- Be cautious while accepting offers such as caller tunes or dialer tunes or open/download emails or attachments from known or unknown sources.
- Be cautious while using Bluetooth in public places as someone may access your confidential data/information.
- Be careful about the websites you are browsing, if it does not look authentic, do not download anything from it.

Glossary

Dictionary of cybersecurity terms:

Adware

Have you ever come across annoying pop-ups with shady or unwanted advertisements on your computer? Such pop-ups are displayed by software called adware. Adware is a software that displays advertisements on your computer. Adware displays advertising banners or pop-ups on your computer when you use an application. This is not necessarily a bad thing. Such advertising can fund the development of useful software, which is then distributed free (for example, Android apps and browser toolbars, many of which are adware funded).

Autorun Worms

These are malicious programs that run via external storage devices. These programs take advantage of the autorun feature of Windows, hence they are known as autorun worms. They execute automatically when the device on which they are stored is plugged into a computer.

Advanced Persistent Threats (APT)

An APT is a type of targeted attack APTs are characterized by an attacker who has time and resources to plan an infiltration into a network. These threats are slow and persistent in their attacks. They infiltrate a targeted network and stay dormant, waiting for the right time to create havoc.

Attack Vector

An attack vector is the carrier or means via which a hacker attacks their targeted systems. It could be an infected email attachment, malicious link, pop-ups, etc.

Anonymizing Proxy

Anonymizing proxies allow the user to hide their web browsing activity. They are often used to bypass web security filters – e.g. to access blocked sites from a work computer. Anonymizing proxies hold security and liability risks for organizations.

Backdoor

Also known as a trapdoor, a backdoor is used by an attacker to gain illegal access to a victim's computer. Backdoor Trojan allows someone to take control of a user's computer without their permission.

Blended Attack

A cyber attack that comprises multiple attack vectors and malware is known as a blended attack. Such attacks usually cause severe damage to targeted systems.

Botnet

Botnet refers to a network of compromised computers that are remotely controlled by a hacker. A botnet is used by a hacker to launch attacks against other targeted victims. Each computer in a botnet is known as a bot or zombie.

Boot Sector Malware

Boot sector malware spreads by modifying the program that enables your computer to start up.

Browser Hijacker

If you find that your Internet browser's settings have changed on its own, including your selected search engine and default homepage, then you have got a browser hijacker in your system.

Brute Force Attack

A brute force attack is one in which hackers try a large number of possible keyword or password combinations to gain unauthorized access to a system or file.

Buffer Overflow

A buffer overflow occurs when a program stores excess data by overwriting other parts of the computer's memory, causing errors or crashes.

Clickjacking

Clickjacking is a technique used by an attacker to inject malicious code in clickable content in websites. Clickjacking is usually done to record the victim's clicks on the Internet or drop a malware infection on the system.

Command and Control Servers

Also called C&C servers or C2, these are machines that an attacker uses to communicate with a botnet (a network of compromised computers) and control the compromised computers in the network.

Content Spoofing

Content spoofing is carried out by an attacker to trick their victims into visiting a fraudulent site that looks like the real one.

Cookie

Cookies are files placed on your computer that allow websites to remember details

Cross Site Scripting (XSS)

Also known as XSS attacks, cross site scripting is a technique used by hackers to plant a malicious code into a genuine website. This allows hackers to gather user's information and use it for nefarious purpose.

Data Leakage

Data leakage is the unauthorized exposure of information. It can result in data theft or data loss.

Data Loss

Data loss is the result of the accidental misplacement of data, rather than its deliberate theft.

Data Theft

Illegal or unauthorized access to or acquisition of classified information or otherwise is termed as data theft i.e. is the deliberate theft of information, rather than its accidental loss.

Denial of Service Attack (DoS)

DoS attacks are targeted attacks against a service to make it inaccessible or unusable by its intended users. Web servers and websites are the common targets of DoS.

Dictionary Attack

In this kind of attack, the hacker tries to break into a password-protected system by trying every combination of word in a dictionary.

DNS Hijacking

The Domain Name System (DNS) is the phone book of the internet. It allows computers to translate website names, like www.google.com, into IP address numbers so that they can communicate with each other.

A DNS hijacking attack changes a computer's settings to either ignore DNS or use a DNS server that is controlled by malicious hackers. The attackers can then redirect communication to fraudulent sites. DNS hijacking is commonly used to redirect users to fake login pages for banks and other online services to steal their login credentials. It can also be used to redirect security sites to non-existent servers to prevent affected users from updating their security software.

Document Malware

Document malware takes advantage of vulnerabilities in applications that let you read or edit documents.

Drive-by Download

If visiting a website or viewing an HTML email automatically downloads a malicious file on your computer, it is known as drive-by download.

E-mail Malware Distribution

E-mail malware refers to malware that is distributed via e-mail.

E-mail Spoofing

E-mail spoofing is how an attacker crafts the header of a malicious e-mail so that user is tricked into viewing it. This technique is typically used in phishing attacks.

E-mail Virus

A computer virus that is delivered to the victim via e-mail is known as an e-mail virus.

Exploit

In most cases, an exploit is defined as an attack where the hacker takes advantage of a security vulnerability in the victim's machine. An exploit takes advantage of a vulnerability in order to access or infect a computer.

Fake anti-virus malware

Fake anti-virus malware reports non-existent threats in order to scare the user into installing malicious software and/or paying for unnecessary product registration and cleanup.

Form Grabber

Malware designed to record sensitive information that the

targeted user provides in forms on the Internet. These malwares particularly target the victim's financial information.

Hacktivism

Hacktivism is the term used to describe hacking activity that's typically for political and social purposes, attacking corporations, governments, organizations and individuals.

Hoax

Hoaxes are reports of false and unsubstantiated claims, in an attempt to trick or defraud users.

Honeypot

A honeypot is a form of trap security specialists use to detect hacking attacks or collect malware samples.

Identity Theft

A menace in the IT security world, identity theft occurs when an attacker gathers personal information and use it to impersonate their victim. This way, the attacker can open illegal bank accounts, obtain credit cards, carry out transactions, etc., using the victim's name.

Internet Worm

Worms are a form of malware that replicates across the Internet or local networks.

Instant Messaging (IM) Worm

Worm are malware that are capable of self-replicating and spreading across the Internet or the compromised network.

Worms that spread via instant messaging networks are called IM worms.

Insider Attack

When someone with an authorized system access carries out malicious activities on a network or a computer, it is known as an insider attack or insider threat. The attacker might be an employee of the targeted business, or an outsider posing as an employee.

Keyloggers

Keylogging is the process of secretly recording keystrokes by an unauthorized third party. Often a part of spyware, keyloggers are used by an attacker to steal sensitive information entered by the user on their keyboard. Keyloggers come in the form of hardware and software.

Likejacking

Likejacking is a part of the clickjacking technique. It usually targets users of the social network community such as Facebook. Scammers share unusual or compelling posts or videos to trick users into liking or sharing them thus, spreading the scam to other users.

Malware

Malware is used as an umbrella term for malicious programs such as viruses, Trojans, worms, spyware, adware, rootkits, ransomware, keyloggers, and rogue security software to name a few. In some cases, the terms 'malware' and 'virus' are used interchangeably.

Man-in-the-Middle Attack

Abbreviated as MITM, this attack is launched by a hacker to intercept, record, and control the communication between two users.

Mobile Phone Virus / Malware

This kind of virus is specifically crafted to run on mobile devices. These viruses can also spread from one infected mobile device to another.

Parasitic Viruses

Parasitic viruses, also known as file viruses, spread by attaching themselves to programs.

Patches

Patches are software add-ons designed to fix software bugs, including security vulnerabilities, in operating systems or applications.

Pharming

Pharming is when a user is redirected to a fake website without their consent or knowledge. In most cases, the fake website looks exactly similar to the actual website that the user intended to visit.

Phishing

Phishing is one of the oldest tricks in the book of hackers. It is a technique used by an attacker to acquire personal information from a victim, by posing as a legitimate organization. Phishing can be executed via spoofed emails, fake phone calls, and even SMSs.

Polymorphic Virus

A polymorphic virus is a malicious program that modifies itself when it replicates. This technique enables it to evade detection by security software.

Potentially unwanted application (PUA)

Potentially unwanted applications are programs that are not malicious but may be unsuitable for use in a business environment, and may create security concerns.

RAT (Remote Access Trojans)

A RAT is a malicious program that can allow a hacker to take over a system from another physical location. Using this malware, the attacker can access and steal confidential and personal data from the infected machine.

Ransomware

Ransomware is a software that denies access to your files or computer until you pay a ransom.

Ransomware is a malicious program that performs the following malicious activities after infecting a computer:

– Makes the system non-functional unless the victim agrees to pay a ransom.

– Encrypts the computer's data and demands a ransom to release it to the victim.

Rogue Antivirus

A rogue antivirus, also known as scareware, is a fake program that disguises itself as a genuine software but performs malicious activities in user's machine. The program may install malware on the system, steal user data, or trick the user to perform fraudulent transactions.

Reverse Social Engineering Attack

In this kind of cyberattack, the attacker convinces a user that they have a problem and that the attacker has a solution to the problem. For instance, an attacker creates a problem for the target. Then the attacker advertises themself as the solution provider, with an intention of luring the victim to divulge sensitive information.

Rootkit

A piece of software that hides programs or processes running on a computer. A rootkit is a program (or a collection of programs) that in itself is not harmful, but helps viruses and malware hide from antivirus software.

Session Hijacking

Session hijacking is an attack wherein a hacker takes control of a computer session to perform illegal activities such as taking over the victim's online accounts.

Shoulder Surfing

Shoulder surfing refers to spying on a user to obtain personal or private information such as PINs, passwords, security codes, etc. Here, the criminal usually looks over a person's shoulder while the latter might be using an ATM, phone or other electronic device.

SMiShing

SMiShing is a type of a phishing attack where targets are sent fake or malicious SMSs. These SMSs are designed to steal personal information from the target, or trick them into visiting a phishing website.

Social Engineering

Social engineering refers to the methods attackers use to deceive victims into performing an action. Typically, these actions are opening a malicious webpage or running an unwanted file attachment.

Social Networking

Social networking websites allow you to communicate and share information. But they can also be used to spread malware and to steal personal information.

Spam

Spam is defined as unwanted or unexpected emails sent in bulk, the electronic equivalent of junk mail, that comes to your inbox. Mostly, spam is used to distribute malware.

Spear Phishing

Spear phishing is a phishing attack where hackers target specific individuals. In a general phishing campaign, phishing emails appear to come from large, well-known organizations.

In spear phishing, however, the email seems to be from a trusted individual or a business that the victim knows about. Today, about 91% of attacks on the Internet consist of spear phishing.

Spoofing (E-Mail)

E-mail spoofing is when the sender address of an e-mail is forged for the purposes of social engineering.

Spyware

A common computer security threat, spyware is a class of malicious program that secretly steals your personal information and sends it to advertisers or hackers. Most spyware come with free online software downloads. Sometimes, a spyware can also come attached with an adware.

SQL Injection

An SQL injection is performed by an attacker to exploit a poorly-designed application to produce unwanted database query results. For instance, an attacker can insert a malicious code into a Web form that is used for user authentication. Via this code, the attacker can send his request to the database and perform illicit activities.

Suspicious files and behaviour

When an endpoint security solution scan files, it labels them as clean or malicious. If a file has a number of questionable characteristics or behaviour, it is labelled as suspicious.

Targeted Attack

A targeted attack is a highly focused attack on specific

individuals or an organization. Hackers use this technique to persistently pursue its target while remaining anonymous, for a long-term period.

Trojan Horse

A Trojan horse is a computer security threat that disguises itself as a harmless program but turns out to be malicious. For instance, a program that appears to be a game but drops a spyware or adware on the user's computer upon activation, is a Trojan horse.

Twishing

Twishing refers to phishing scams that are carried over Twitter. The attacker might tweet a post interesting or strange enough to trick users into visiting a fraudulent website and logging in with their credentials.

URL Spoofing

A technique used by hackers to create a fake URL that impersonates the URL of a secure or legitimate website. A spoofed URL looks exactly like the one of the original websites, but redirects users to a phishing or a malicious site.

Virus

Virus is a malicious program usually attached to a legitimate or harmless program. When the program runs, the virus gets executed and performs activities that harm infected machines and their data. A virus can copy itself and spread to other files.

Vishing

Vishing is a phishing attack wherein a hacker uses voice calls to trick users into divulging personal or financial information. Vishing attacks are carried out using conventional phone systems or Voice over Internet Procotol (VoIP) systems.

Vulnerability

A vulnerability, also known as a security vulnerability, is a flaw or error in a software or operating system that can let hackers take control of the affected machine and use it for illegal activities.

Wabbit

A wabbit is malicious program that keeps dropping its duplicate copies on the infected system. Unlike a worm, it does not spread across networks.

Website Spoofing

Website spoofing refers to creating a fake site that looks exactly like a trusted and popular website, in order to collect personal or financial information from users. Spoofed websites are created using legitimate logos, colors, designs, etc., to make them look realistic.

Whale Phishing

Whale phishing is a campaign that is aimed particularly at wealthier individuals. It is also known as whaling.

Worm

A worm is a stand-alone malware that can self-replicate itself. Unlike a virus, it does not require a 'host program' to attach itself to. It spreads by placing its functional copies in email attachments, instant messages, networks, flash drives, etc. A worm can be used to distribute Trojans, viruses, spam, phishing emails, and other forms of malware.

Zero-day Vulnerability

A zero-day vulnerability refers to a security flaw that does not have a fix yet, and can be exploited by hackers at any given time. In most cases, hackers try to find a vulnerability that neither developers nor users are aware of. And before they do, hackers develop an exploit (a malicious code) to take advantage of the flaw.

Zombie

A zombie refers to a computer that has been taken over by a hacker. Hackers usually create a large group of zombie computers called botnet, to launch their attacks.

Think Before You Post

People have a habit of behaving differently online than they do in person – the large audience is invisible, so may feel protected by their screens. This can be a positive thing, like someone feeling more confident to open up and be themselves. But sometimes people will misuse social networks to shame and bully others.

Posting online is instant, public and more often than not, permanent. Remember, **The Internet is Written in PEN not PENCIL**. Once you post, you lose all control of what happens to it – it only takes one friend to share it on their own profiles for it to be completely out of your hands.

Too often young people are finding their posts coming back to haunt them. Universities, future employers and schools can easily find a trial of your online identity. If they don't like what they see, it can mean a serious loss of opportunity. You may even find yourself in trouble with the police.

The cyber world is the **REAL** world with **REAL** consequences.

People don't think twice before posting opinions on networking websites like Facebook and Twitter, especially when it comes to social and political happenings around us. So, the arrest of a Mumbai girl Shaheen Dhada over her post on Facebook, questioning the shutdown in the city for Shiv Sena patriarch Bal Thackeray's funeral, came as a shock and surprise for many. Shaheen's friend Renu was also arrested for 'liking' and sharing her comment. The girls were then arrested on the grounds of the IPC section 295-A and 505-2 and, of course the IT Act 2008. The sections 295-A and 505-2 are concerned with the crime of hurting religious sentiments and outraging castes and races whereas the IT Act 2008 is concerned with the issues related to the cyber security of the country. It was later realized that police had charged them under wrong sections. However, the girls were later released a few days later after protest all around the city and filing of petitions in the court.

Now my question is when all these get to read in the newspaper then no worry about it but when they come in touch of social sites then this is called a crime.

Considering that the social networking websites are a 'free space' to share, circulate and discuss issues, rarely do the netizens, especially the youngsters, expect police at their doorsteps for posting a comment on the virtual world.

Sharing much too much: It's about time we realize that not everything we do in our life needs to be documented online. Many of us have become addicted to documenting practically every breath we take on social media. Is it any wonder that "overshare" was The Chambers Dictionary's word of the year in 2014? Everyone needs to understand the importance of social sharing for your platform – versus oversharing for your ego.

Sharing inappropriate material: The Internet is unforgiving. Before texting, tweeting, emailing, posting or sharing anything consider how you'd feel if your words or images went viral. Is your human need for approval, for eliciting likes and retweets, driving you to share questionable material? Does the content convey how you truly want to be perceived? You should have zero expectation of privacy when it comes to cyberspace.

Sharing with wrong people: You should frequently review the settings on your social media accounts and make sure you actually know who you are connecting with. Who's in your social media friends and mobile contact lists? Do you actually know them? Would be embarrassed if you accidentally but dialled one of them? Just because you've set your privacy settings as high as possible doesn't mean you are 100 percent secure from trolls or a friend turned foe. You may believe that you're only sharing this with your core group, but remember, you don't always have control over what photos others choose to take and share.

Sharing in haste: People often refer to the phrase, "Think before you post." I say, "Pause,". It only takes a second to post – and 6 seconds to pause. Take that minute to consider that post before you hit send. Picture yourself in that photo or receiving that e-mail. Is this something that could be embarrassing or humiliating at a later date? Does it reveal too much information? Always ask the permission of others who are in the photo, especially with children, before posting it, and never assume that they have given you permission unless they have. If we've heard it once, we've heard it a million times – think before you post – but that hasn't stopped many of us from making digital blunders.

Sharing without dignity: When we see adults, politicians, celebrities or athletes acting childish or bullish online, it sends the wrong message to our fellow adults and to our kids. Many of these pople are role models who our youths look up to.

Sharing with negativity: I'm sure everyone knows people who use their social media feed as a venting machine. The complaining never stops, whether it's their bleak life, their horrible job, or their dismal dating scene. Worse is when they impose their negative thoughts on your good fortune – you've just landed your dream job, and they make an unenthusiastic remark line, "Not a great company to work for." Yes, we've all experienced the Negative Nellies and Debbie Downers in our world, and we don't want to be one of them—especially online. From the moment you are given the privilege of your first keyboard, your virtual résumé begins. It's up to you to maintain and create a positive persona. It's true, we can't be happy all the time, and it's fine to reach out for support in times of grief. But the good news about the Internet, and even your smartphone, is that you can turn it off if you're having a bad day. Also, never post something in haste or anger that you might later regret—log off instead. I like to say, "**When in doubt, click out**." Remember, once you post a comment, a thought or a picture, it is on the internet forever. No matter what you do, you can never totally erase it. Also, if you hurt someone, you cannot change that fact either. Bottom line, online posting can have very serious negative impacts on your life or other people's lives that you are not intending to hurt.

About the Author

Rakhi R Wadhwani is an information security, privacy, risk and compliance consultant.

Information is a critical business asset, and businesses must ensure that it is accurate, appropriately safeguarded and available only to those authorized to use it.

Information assurance and compliance programs must be built and implemented using a business-oriented approach to be most successful and effective. These programs help organizations comply with an ever-increasing number of national and international laws and regulations, encourage IT departments to communicate and work harmoniously with other business units, minimize risks to sensitive company and personal information, and make personnel aware of how to work more effectively while safeguarding information.

She is an Associate Member of National Cyber Safety and Security Standards, Certified Information Security Consultant (CISC), Certified Professional Forensic Analyst (CPFA) and Certified Professional Hacker (CPHNxG) and also Associate Editor in Digital 4n6 Journal

Her skills and know-how encompass Information risk management and compliance, Security controls, Compliance and Technical audits, Business Continuity Management, Vulnerability Management and Information Protection and Data Loss Prevention.

Her articles are published in various magazines, leading newspaper and technical blogs.

She can be invited for delivering session on Information Security, Social Media etc.

Contact of the Author:

E-Mail : academiic.arista@gmail.com

Twitter: @AcademiicArista

Facebook: https://www.facebook.com/AcademiicAristaOfficial/

Made in United States
Troutdale, OR
11/03/2026

56844384R00194